MY MOTHER'S DAUGHTER

MY MOTHER'S DAUGHTER

Enid Richemont

HUTCHINSON
London Sydney Auckland Johannesburg

To Jude with love

Copyright © Enid Richemont 1990
All rights reserved

The right of Enid Richemont to be identified as author of this
work has been asserted by Enid Richemont in accordance with the
Copyright, Designs and Patent Acts 1988

First published in 1990 by
Hutchinson Children's Books
An imprint of the Random Century Group Ltd
20 Vauxhall Bridge Road, London SW1V 2SA

Random Century Australia (Pty) Ltd
20 Alfred Street, Milsons Point, Sydney, NSW 2016

Random Century New Zealand Ltd
PO Box 40–086, Glenfield, Auckland 10, New Zealand

Random Century South Africa (Pty) Ltd
PO Box 337, Bergvlei 2012, South Africa

Photoset by Speedset, Ellesmere Port
Printed and bound in Great Britain by
Mackays of Chatham PLC, Chatham, Kent

British Library Cataloguing in Publication Data
Richemont, Enid
My mother's daughter
I. Title
823'.914 [J]

ISBN 00–917422–70–6

1

I keep my hair in a plastic bag inside my aunt's chest of drawers. Where do you keep yours?

Ever seen a bagful of human hair? Looks a bit like one of those shapeless furry animals you adopt when you're a little kid. Sometimes I think it's going to grow two wicked little shiny button eyes – amber, with black centres – and stare right back at me. I should stuff the whole lot inside a cushion – preferably one of those Laura Ashley jobs with lace and flowers – and send it off to my mum. As a keepsake. A souvenir: FROM YOUR LOVING DAUGHTER CECILIA. That'd be a joke. . . .

You see, that's the way she'd like me – clean, fluffed-up and stuffed inside a pretty parcel so I couldn't answer back. She could keep me like that indefinitely, show me off to all her friends: 'Look at my daughter . . . such a lovely design. . . .'

I won't do it, though. I mean, I won't send it to her – what a waste! That hair is mine. Was. Well, the stuff was part of me, wasn't it? I couldn't let them just sweep it into the bin and throw it away. Hard to believe, now, that not long ago it was growing on my head and curling over my shoulders, all ringlets, like a judge's wig. Pre-Raphaelite, my mother called it.

1

I called it shit.

Does that word offend you?

Why should I bother to ask? You're not real. I made you up. I needed somebody. Who else can I talk to in this rotten dump?

It's great, making people up. I used to do it when I was little. I used to do it at primary school, in the days before Ranjit, when no one would play with me. Listen, I could make you into anyone: someone of my own age, a best friend (I could never talk like this to Ranjit, going on about my mum, baring my soul, that sort of thing – it would just embarrass her). Perhaps I ought to make you much older – someone wise and mature, tough and experienced; someone who's done it all, really lived. Not a bloke. Men never listen. You'll have to be a woman. But not like her. Not like my mother. Life has to be sanitized for my mum: cleaned up, prettied and preferably framed. She may dirty her fingers with charcoal, but never with reality.

I ought to give you a name. What would you like? Jenny? Liz? I'd respect your choice. She wouldn't. Names are important. I should know.

You can call me Cealie – why not? Everyone else does, except my aunt who calls me Sam, but she is dotty and doesn't count.

Cealie is not my real name. The kids in my old primary school made it up, and it's stuck ever since. How perceptive of you: yes, it DID start off as 'Silly' – how did you guess? 'Silly, silly, silly Cecilia. . . .' Well, why not? What do you do with a name like that if you have a six-year-old's sense of humour? Silly? You bet! Didn't I look it, with my Tweetie-pie ringlets and all those 'interesting' clothes Mum used to make for me?

2

My mother, if you must know, is Freda Thomson.

Now I don't suppose that means a thing to you unless you notice the names of the people who do pictures for kids' books, or look at the backs of greetings cards to see who made up the design. You will have heard of 'The Rainbow Kingdom', though. I mean, everyone has. Most people think of it as just another television serial for kids, but there is a book. Not hers. She can't write – she just does the pictures. Open it. Surprise, surprise: see my prissy features and my sickly curls. Princess Daisy – yes, that's me . . . the heroine! Except that the real one had a hell of a lot more fun.

How could my mother do it to me?

Easily . . . you don't know my mum.

I model for the lady; have done since I was a baby. My sister does too.

Don't get any fancy ideas about that. Sitting still for hours dressed up like a dog's dinner is no joke, but if your mum's an artist, that is something you get stuck with.

Even Mum calls me Cealie now.

Did. . . .

It was Ranjit, clever girl, who changed my name, my nickname, gentling it into something more acceptable.

Ranjit has this whispery voice and long plaits like something out of one of those old-fashioned school-girl stories, but her brother is a Black Belt and her dad carves people up in the Heath Hospital. She has influence. I will never understand why she took me on. Sometimes I think she saw me as a one-girl minority group, to be protected. When she made herself into my friend, I didn't complain. She was a

3

sweet girl and I needed a friend. Not much she can do for me now, though. This one I have to get through alone.

Somewhere I read that you are born alone and you die alone. I don't know much about dying but the bit about being born is rubbish – your mother has to be around even then.

Well, that's all over for me. For her, too.

Five days ago, she threw me out.

I didn't realize how angry I was. We're middle class, you see. We talk things through. We don't go in for screaming rows in my family.

I didn't realize how much I hated her.

I enjoyed that row. Yes, I did – every minute of it. It excited me like a storm excites me. There's a kind of terrible purity about a storm, with the sky all raging and weeping around you, and then, when it's all over, the air is light and clear and you can see for miles and miles. . . .

It had been boiling away inside me for weeks, months, years, probably, but it was sparked off, I suppose, by that idiotic conversation I overheard in the school lavatory. Which was odd. I mean, it was nothing new. I'd heard it all before. In some form or another, I'd been hearing it all my life.

'See Princess Daisy at the disco last night?'

'All that hair. . . .'

My stomach contracted. It was me they were talking about, of course. Who else?

'Who's a pretty girl then?' Snigger, snigger.

And who else, I thought bitterly, had a portrait of herself: Cecilia, aged ten, ringlets crawling like caterpillars out of an Alice band – simpering from above the fireplace, for all the world to see?

4

Afterwards, walking home with Ranjit, the words just fell out of me. 'I'm going to have it all chopped off.'

'All *what* chopped off?'

'My hair, stupid. I'm having it cut. Really short.'

'I don't believe it.'

'Why not? Why shouldn't I?'

Then she called my bluff. 'When?'

What could I say? 'Today, actually. This afternoon.'

'Where are you getting it done?'

I wanted to shock. 'Shavers,' I said.

I waited for the reaction, and when it came, it was totally satisfactory. 'Shavers?' Ranjit shrieked. 'You crazy?'

'When I said short,' I said coolly, 'I meant it!' I was enjoying myself, not taking myself seriously, teasing her.

'Your mum know?'

She should not have said that.

'Not her hair, is it?' I snapped.

Ranjit sighed. 'My mother'd kill me. . . .' There was a small note of envy in her voice. Then she recovered. 'A woman's chief beauty lies in her hair . . .' and she fingered the thick, glossy plaits which reached down to her waist.

'I do what I please.'

'You're not serious!'

'Wait and see.'

I was committed. There was no going back.

Not a bad way to change things, I thought at the time: declare your intentions to someone and then you're honour bound to carry them through.

Playing with the scissors, I considered my re-

5

flection in the bathroom mirror. I could have done the job myself, but the prospect of hacking away like a delinquent two-year-old did not appeal. I could have asked my sister, Roz, but she was round at a friend's house. Roz wouldn't have touched it anyway; she'd have chickened out.

Besides, I wanted something trendy.

My resolution was strengthened by a treasure trove of three forgotten fivers stashed away inside a teapot. It was a sign. A portent. And I could soon pay it back, I thought – with that Saturday job almost lined up.

Anyway, Mum owed me for modelling.

'I'm going out,' I called. She was working upstairs.

'OK, but don't be late. . . .' Her voice tailed off; she was already thinking about something else.

It was funny: even the punk hairdresser in Camden Town tried to talk me out of it, as if I were committing some sort of strange crime, as if the stuff didn't really belong to me at all.

Later, my hair in a bag (they gave it to me all gift wrapped and fastened at the top with one of those silver hair-clips), I rode home on the bus. My head felt conspicuously light, exposed, naked. My fingers kept straying over the soft stubble and that solitary tuft on my forehead. For the first time in my life, I was aware of having ears – I could feel them. And, shadowed across the driver's broad back, I could see my face, the shape of my head, and it was like the head of a young monk – all clean lines and no fuss. I liked what I saw.

The defiance I felt, going into the house, was almost religious. I felt high. I felt elated.

But my mother, as usual, messed the whole thing up.

6

'Cealie! Oh my God! What happened to you?'

I shrugged. 'Just had my hair cut. People do, you know. . . .'

'Oh my God! You look awful!'

I played it cool. 'I like it this way.'

She began to gibber. She always does when she's upset. 'Who . . . did it to you? Not Ranjit, surely?'

That really made me fall about.

'Ranjit? Ranjit?' I screamed. 'You must be joking! Listen – this was a professional job. I went to the hairdresser's. . . .'

'My God, I'll sue!'

'You can't.'

'What kind of a. . .?'

'Shavers.' It was a lovely word and I pronounced it with satisfaction.

She simmered down a bit. 'Why didn't you tell me?'

'Do I have to tell you everything?'

She sighed. 'Look, if you wanted to be more fashionable . . .' This was it – the understanding bit. I steeled up.

'Don't tell me – I know. You would have arranged it all for me, made me an appointment at some place for middle-aged trendies, and then you would have hung around, flapping and fussing, asking for something not too extreme for your little girlie . . . telling them what to do. . . .'

'I care about you.' I could hear the choke in her voice, and I couldn't bear it. 'What's so wrong about that?'

'Nothing . . . I mean, everything. Oh, don't you see?' I suddenly wanted to cry myself.

'But this was important. . . .'

7

'To you, yes. What about me?'

She was immediately defensive. 'What is that supposed to mean?'

'It means that I'm not your pretty-pretty poodle any more!'

'I've never treated you –'

'That's what you think.'

She simmered down. 'This is silly. Of both of us. What's done's done.' She walked around me, biting her lips, squeezing out a compromise. 'I suppose,' she said finally, 'there's no real harm done. It'll grow out. . . .'

That did it.

'Then I'll have it re-done!' I shouted. 'Listen – it cost me fifteen quid. Not much for all that work – like clipping a hedge, the man said. And you paid for it! It was your money. Just thought you'd like to know.'

I could hear the knife-edge in my voice, slashing into her, hurting her. Why didn't she stop me? I wanted her to stop me. One slap and I would have burst into tears – she must have known that. But all I got was an ice-cold question.

'Where did you get it?'

Who did she think she was? The police?

'Inside Gran's teapot on the dresser,' I said. 'You shouldn't be so careless. . . .'

'Get out!'

She was the one who said it.

I just obeyed. After all, she left me no choice.

Upstairs in my room, I pulled down an old duffel bag and began packing it methodically with the basics: clean knickers and socks, the optimistic bra she'd bought me for my undersized boobs, a jumper and shorts and a spare pair of jeans. I rolled up a sleeping bag left over from some camping trip – it might come in useful. I felt totally calm, as if this move had been quietly planned months ago, not forced on me like that. On the way out, I even remembered to pick up my toothbrush, and a box of tampons from the bathroom cupboard.

When I left, I slammed the front door.

I wasn't angry any more.

I just wanted her to know that I had gone.

2

Before I had got halfway to the tube, my rocket of defiance had fizzled into a damp squib. I had no money and nowhere to go.

And my splendid walk-out began to feel uncomfortably like one of those childhood escapades – you know the sort of thing. You say: I'm never coming back, and you set up your little camp on the street corner, with a cushion, an old blanket and a bag of crisps, and then you cave in over something silly like a need to go to the loo. I had to remind myself that this was different; that I was nearly sixteen, not a kid, and that surrender could not be bought so easily. After all, I had some resources – friends, connections. . . . I could even sleep rough for a night or two, on the Heath, under a bush. The weather was good, the nights were warm, and I wasn't scared.

I mean, who'd want to rape me? Anyway, newspapers always exaggerate things.

Besides, I could spend the first night at Ranjit's. I'd done it before.

Ranjit, I knew, would help if she could: she always did. It would be fun, anyway, to show off my new self to my correct little friend who was so delightfully shockable. I walked across the High Street and into the Close.

Counting on her mum to be in the kitchen, I rang the bell.

Ranjit screamed. 'Your hair!'

'Sssh!' I said, turning round slowly, savouring her reaction.

'Fantastic,' she whispered. 'Awful! Cool!'

'Said I would.'

'I wouldn't dare. Your mum seen it?'

I nodded. 'And she didn't exactly approve. In fact . . .' I paused for dramatic effect, 'she's thrown me out!'

A small frown of puzzlement grew between Ranjit's thick brows. 'I don't understand.'

'It's simple. She's thrown me out, told me to go, to get out, not to come back. . . .'

Ranjit shook her head. 'Mothers do not do such things.'

'Well, mine does.'

Her mum called out, 'Who's that?'

'Cealie.'

The smell from the kitchen was making me feel hungry.

'You have homework to do.' Ranjit's mum is strict. 'Not too much gossip-gossip.'

Upstairs we fell about laughing.

'She didn't see.'

'Wait till she does. Hey! Got something to eat?'

'I'll see what I can do.'

Ranjit came back with a plate of samosas and two cans of Coke, and we shared them, sitting on her bed. She didn't say much. I knew Ranjit. Something was bothering her, and it wasn't just my hair.

11

'But she's nice, your mum,' she said at last. 'I mean, she wouldn't do a thing like that. You go back and tell her you're sorry.'

'But I'm not.'

Ranjit sighed. 'It doesn't matter. I mean – you've won, haven't you? She can't make you go and stick it all back on your head, can she?'

I fumbled about in my jacket pocket and came up with a mangled cigarette.

'Share a smoke?'

We pushed up the window to conceal the smell, knocking the ash on to the greasy plate. Ranjit giggled. 'She'd kill me,' she said.

I ground the fag-end into a sooty mess and flipped it into the garden below.

'I'm not going back,' I said. 'Look.' I opened up my duffel bag and showed her the sleeping bag to prove I meant business.

'Where will you go?'

'I don't know yet. I'll find something. Look – do you think I could spend the night here?'

Ranjit frowned. 'If it was just me I'd say yes, but my parents would not allow it.'

'I've done it before. . . .'

'It's not that. What would they say if your mother or your father rang us?'

'That they hadn't seen me.'

'My parents couldn't lie like that.'

'OK then, you don't have to tell them, do you? I could hide, couldn't I?'

'Where?'

I looked round. There were cupboards. There was a built-in wardrobe. There was plenty of space under her bed.

12

But Ranjit still shook her head.

Sometimes that girl really irritates me – she won't do anything.

I snapped. 'Alright, then, since you're such a goody-goody, I'll leave. I can take care of myself. Thanks for your bloody help. Thanks for nothing!'

'Wait,' she pleaded, not wanting to lose face. 'Listen – I've got an idea. What about Pauline?'

'What about Pauline?' Pauline was a year older than us and I hardly knew her. Anyway, she'd left school months ago.

'She and Bill are in a squat in Stoke Newington. You could probably sleep there.'

'Oh, sure . . . three in a bed?'

'Don't be silly. It's a big place: there'll be other people there. They asked my brother to a party and he told me. I can find their address – it'll be in his book.'

She ran off, anxious to please.

I wanted to leave, but it was difficult, so I sat on the bed and waited.

When she came back she was waving a scrap of paper. 'Got it!'

I shrugged. 'So what?'

'They might help.'

'I'll think about it,' I said icily.

'You got any money?'

'Not much.'

'Here. . . .' She opened a tin box, took out a couple of notes and pressed them into my hand. 'Pay me back one day.'

It was embarrassing; I'd been so bitchy.

'Thanks,' I said in an off-hand kind of way.

'I think you ought to go home.'

13

I laughed.

'Cheers,' I said. 'See you sometime. . . .'

The directions on the piece of paper were basic but good – after all, Bakshi had made it to that party. They allowed him more freedom, but then he was a boy. Men, I thought: they always get a better deal.

I sat on the bus, watching the streets rolling backwards, all those familiar places falling into the past and nothing for me to do but go on.

After a long walk, I found it. Most of the houses in that street were being squatted. This one had a snake pattern in pink and green painted over its front, and in its garden a crazy lettuce, its lime-white stem speckled with yellow, was growing about a mile high. Most of the windows had been boarded up but the front door was wide open.

'THATCHER OUT' and 'NO NUKES' had been sprayed in scarlet across one of the stone steps. I moved tentatively around the greasy skeleton of a motorbike whose black and oily guts were spread out over a newspaper in the hall. The warm, still air simmered with the distant sound of heavy rock music. Timidly, like Bluebeard's wife, I tried the first room. It stank of raw onion.

I called out: 'Pauline?'

The girl who was chopping vegetables at the sink turned and offered me a tear-stained smile.

'Hi,' she said vaguely. 'Can't see you properly – who is it? Come on in.'

'It's Cealie.'

'Who?'

'Cealie Thomson.'

People were nestled on an old mattress, smoking

14

and drinking mugs of tea. I recognized Bill down there, Pauline's boyfriend for years – almost a marriage, people said.

Pauline came over and peered at me. She had changed. Her long hair had been cut short and bleached, and her mauve eye-shadow was messy with tears.

'Cealie Thomson? My God, so it is! Whatever happened to all the hair?'

'Had it cut.'

'Had it cut? That must the understatement of the year! Hey, Bill – it's Cealie Thomson and she's had it all off!'

Bill uncurled himself languidly and walked over to examine me, putting a finger under my chin and moving my head about, this way and that, frowning, pursing his lips, playing the art critic. His touch bothered me. He had slick, dark hair and a pale, masochistic face, and I had once, when I was much younger, had a thing about him.

'Prefer it the way it was. . . .'

Pauline sighed. 'Men are so conservative. It's certainly – different. Yes, I think it quite suits you. Shows off your bone structure, which isn't bad; makes you look less of a kid. . . .'

Her attitude irritated me. Hair on, hair off, was I still nothing but an object to be gawped at? A prize poodle at a show?

'Look,' I snapped, 'the haircut's not important. I need somewhere to sleep tonight – my family's chucked me out.' This, surely, would be something Pauline would understand; people said she'd gone through hell with her lot after dropping out of school and moving in with Bill.

15

'My God, Cealie – whatever did you do?' Her apparent concern was spiked, I felt, with amusement.

I tried to play it cool.

'Nothing much, really,' I said. 'Just wanted a bit of independence and she – I mean, they – couldn't take it. The usual reason,' I added, feeling sort of philosophical and worldly wise. 'The haircut sort of clinched things. I'll sort it out . . . probably get myself a job. . . .'

'You'll be lucky.'

'But just now things are a bit difficult,' I persisted, ignoring her. 'Ranjit gave me your address. She thought you might. . . .'

'So you want to doss down here?'

'Just for a day or two, yes, if you've got the space.'

'Plenty of floor. Got a sleeping bag?'

'Of course.' I still felt quite proud of the way I had organized my getaway.

'Dump your stuff then. Want a cuppa?'

I was in. I had made it.

I moved my head. It felt light, clean, uncluttered. A small shiver of excitement ran through me. I had never thought it would work out so well. I had never thought I could pull it off. Now I had broken all the rules and I was out there on my own.

It was scary.

Scary, but breathtaking . . .

3

I lay on the mattress in my zipped-open sleeping bag, watching the lights of passing cars flickering like an old movie over the dark walls, listening to voices in the street, hoping the others had remembered to bolt the front door. Above my head, squeaking springs and muffled cries suggested somebody's sexual activity, and I found myself asking, with guilty curiosity – whose?

The mattress was lumpy and sagged in the middle. It smelt musty and intimate, in a way nothing ever did at home. The middle classes, I thought, deodorize everything.

And I wondered what they'd be doing now, my nice, respectable family; if my dad had rung the police; if Roz was scared or impressed; if my mother had been able to sleep. Bet she's sorry she said it, I thought. Bet she's crying. . . .

Well, too bad.

We had stayed up until nearly three, talking, smoking, drinking and listening to music. Around midnight people from the top of the house drifted in with a couple of friends. I passed out and woke up later with my head in someone's lap. A guy was fooling round with a guitar, plucking a stringful of

17

random chords.

I could hear Pauline going on about her parents.

'They are so incredibly static . . . I mean, wanting me to go through the whole middle-class thing, just like they did. You know, university, good job (they don't seem to have heard of graduate unemployment), and after all that, with their permission, I'd be allowed to consider a commitment. . . .' She laughed and ran her fingers through Bill's sleek hair. 'Well, I've got my commitment so stuff the rest of it. People are what matter to me. They don't seem to get that.'

'Bunch of Thatcherites . . . what do you expect? The only things that mean anything at all to them are money and whatever they call success.'

'Nothing wrong with money. . . .'

'Money? Show me some – I've forgotten what it looks like.'

'What about Cealie's lot? Changes her hairstyle and they turf her out.'

'Bunch of bleeding fascists. . . .'

'Isn't your mum an artist?' someone asked. 'Thought they were supposed to be more broad-minded and tolerant than the rest of us.'

Tolerant? That was a joke.

'Listen,' I said, 'they're worse, if anything. . . .' I was just awake, slightly tipsy and relaxed as butter. 'Ever considered what happens when a so-called creative person goes and has a kid. It's just a little bit of raw material for expressing himself through. And – you know something?' They were all listening to me. I felt great. 'Most of the time they don't even know they're doing it. And – I mean – you can't tell them; they wouldn't know what you were talking about.'

I was impressing even myself.

'Do you know,' I went on angrily, 'she's got a pen-and-ink drawing of me over the fireplace. Me, aged ten . . . Alice in bloody Wonderland. . . .'

My voice tailed away and I lost the point of what I was saying. Suddenly I found myself engulfed by an unexpected wave of sadness and I began to cry, silently. I could feel the tears rolling down my cheeks but in the candlelight no one seemed to notice or care.

'So what are you going to do?'

I mopped my face with the back of my hand. 'Hay fever,' I explained, cleverly. I gulped and felt better. 'I don't know really. Lie low for a bit, I suppose – I mean, there's bound to be a flap. Then I'll look for a job or go on Social Security.'

'Job might be a problem – always supposing you find one,' said Pauline. 'A bit under age, aren't you?'

'I'm nearly sixteen,' I said defensively.

'Under age until you're sixteen. Parents' property . . . you know, all that crap. And don't forget – they'll report you missing.'

'But they chucked me out,' I said weakly.

'Could have changed their minds by now, had second thoughts. People do. . . .'

'Could always go back . . . turn up on the doorstep. Big reconciliation scene: come home, Cealie; all is forgiven.'

'No, thanks.'

'And what about your exam results?'

'What exam results?'

'O levels. Or did you opt out of those too?'

They were already behind me; years, it felt, behind me.

'I couldn't care less,' I said, and it was true; I couldn't. 'Just bits of paper. . . .'

'You could come with us, I suppose. . . .' The girl who was speaking was called Martha; she was plump and pretty, with soft cow's eyes. 'It would get you out of London, at least. We're hitching down to Wales to stay with Tom's brother for a week or so; then we're planning to camp out, further west.'

'Oh, but I couldn't do that. . . .' Even I could see that the atmosphere was unreal; that we were all a bit pissed; that offers like that were like coloured balloons at a kid's party – attractive but transient.

She went on organizing me. I didn't mind: I didn't take it seriously.

'Get yourself a job down at Porthcawl – why not? Plenty of seaside jobs going and not too many questions asked.'

'My mother's lot come from down there,' I said. 'My gran lives near Swansea.'

'So what? How often does your gran go to the beach?'

'I've even got this dotty great-aunt up in the Black Mountains. . . .' I can't think what made me mention her.

'Sounds like a witch.'

I grinned. 'Nothing so promising. Just senile, I think. I wouldn't know. Haven't seen her since I was a little kid . . . she's about a hundred and fifty years old at least.'

I put the offer out of my mind. By morning, I thought, she would be having second thoughts about it; if she remembered making it in the first place, which was by no means certain. Anyway, I didn't want to be a hanger-on.

Funny, though, I thought, that they should be going to that particular place – that familiar, well-worn backdrop to our duty visits to Gran – the chips and candyfloss beach to which you could always escape when the stuffiness of that little terraced house became unbearable. It would be the last place on earth my family would look for me; my relationship with my grandmother is not what you would call close. The more I thought about it, the more attractive the idea became. I didn't have to stay around them, did I? Once I had got myself sorted out. . . .

I considered chickening out of the whole thing, giving up, going home – it would be so easy. Already I was feeling guilty about Mum. I mean, I don't like hurting people. It wasn't too late to hop on the early morning bus and turn up on the doorstep with the milk. I imagined the relief, the tears, the hugs, then the anger. The anger I could take, but not the talking-it-through, not the full-blown analysis – what gives her the idea she's got a right to my soul?

No, I said. No. My soul's my own, thank you very much. I've wriggled out of that airtight little box called Family. I am Me now. Whatever Me is.

And if I was jumping out of one box and into another . . .? Well, that was a risk I would have to take.

I drifted into a half-dream, moving from box to box, no two ever quite the same, until I passed into a heavy slumber which lasted until early afternoon. Then someone was shaking me awake.

Thick with sleep, I propped myself up on one elbow. Sunlight was gilding the dirt on the cracked window-panes and fingering the motes of dust that danced in the shadows. A neglected spider plant drooped against the light.

21

'Have some cornflakes.' Someone dumped an open packet, a chipped china bowl and a bottle half full of milk on the floor beside me.

'Thanks.'

I mixed myself a milky mess and began spooning it up. Somewhere in the room a bluebottle was droning its summer prayer. My head ached. I needed some strong coffee but all they had was tea.

'Look, I don't want to push you into anything but. . . .'

'We've got to get going.'

'Grab your things if you're coming.'

'Great weather to be by the sea,' Pauline added brightly. 'Wouldn't mind coming along with you.' At that moment it was quite clear, even in my hung-over state, that she was washing her hands of me. I didn't blame her: I was a liability. Why should she care? We may have gone to the same primary school, but that doesn't constitute a relationship.

And they were serious.

I made up my mind.

'Sounds fantastic,' I said quickly. 'I'll just sort out my stuff.'

'Sure you wouldn't rather go home?'

'You must be joking.' It was the point of abandon, of no possible return.

I had never hitch-hiked before. My mother, I thought gleefully, would have been horrified.

We lettered up a placard, 'TO THE WEST', and bussed it up to the North Circular Road. At the junction we stood like a bunch of whores, waving our arms at passing cars and trying to look pleasing. The traffic sped past us as if we had the plague, but finally a small green van pulled up alongside.

22

'Going far?'

'South Wales.'

'You're in luck. Hop in. Students, are you?'

I suppose you could have called us that. Students? Why not? Sounded good.

Tom's lie, 'That's right,' brought an instant response.

'Son's a student. Never any money, poor sod . . . better off on the dole . . . know what it's like. . . .' His coarse, purplish-ruddy features glowed with awareness of his own generosity. 'After summer jobs, I suppose?'

We nodded.

'Where you looking?'

'Dunno . . . Swansea, Porthcawl. . . .'

'Trying for a suntan,' I added feebly.

'Costa Brava's what you need for that, not bloody Swansea. Drop you off at Newport if that's any use to you.'

'That's great!'

It was funny. Last night I'd been imagining how it might be and this was it. This was real. Huddled together with Tom and Martha inside the dark, doggy-smelling tunnel of the van, squatting among the scattered tools, the torn newspapers, the rags and old cardboard boxes, I found that the journey was taking on an almost hypnotic quality. Real? I wasn't sure any more, as I sat, watching the landscape endlessly dividing, parting, and the bridges rhythmically swallowing the grey-and-white tongue of the motorway. I felt like a dreamer trapped inside his own dream, or an actor frozen for ever inside his own play.

Our driver, his good deed done, fumbled with a

few disintegrating sandwiches and turned for solace to Radio One. He seemed to have forgotten about us. Crows cut black paper silhouettes against a vast blue sky. We didn't talk much.

Tipped, at length, on to the scrubby grass of a service station, we watched the back of our van melting into the stream of traffic.

'Well, that's that,' said Tom.

We stocked up with chocolate and ice-cream and settled down to wait, wedging our placard between the bags. The hot, glittery afternoon had mellowed into evening gold. Behind us lay the Great Divide of the Severn Bridge, where Roz and I once used to squabble over which of us should play the toll man. She's not a bad kid, my little sister. I was going to miss her.

After about an hour we were picked up by a loquacious chicken farmer in an old Ford Escort. Martha came pretty close to sabotaging that, with loud complaints about battery hens – I mean, I don't disagree with her, but there's a time and a place for everything. After a while, though, even she managed to gag her principles in favour of avoiding a thirty mile trek.

We took a bus to the housing estate where Tom's brother lived. His wife, June, came to the door. She wore a turquoise cotton sundress. A naked toddler hid behind a fistful of skirt.

'There's a surprise – thought you were Martin home early.' She sounded disappointed. 'Didn't think you'd get here so soon – come on in.' Her pale eyes were dull with fatigue.

'There's lovely the weather is. . . .' She said it automatically – a meaningless greeting which she

24

offered to everyone. 'Hope it keeps up like this for you.'

The roots of her bleached hair were mouse-brown, and the backs of her plump legs, as she turned away, were scorched pink from the sun. I wondered how old she was.

A little girl with brown curly hair and a frilly sunsuit trotted out of the kitchen and climbed into Tom's lap. June came back with teapot, cups and a plate of fairy cakes on a flowered tray.

'There's a little flirt you are. Loves her Uncle Tom.'

The toddler, confined to a high chair, fought a messy battle over food.

'Advantage of summer . . . don't have to bother much about clothes for them,' said June, spooning a creamy goo into his protesting mouth. 'Once over with a flannel and they're as good as new.'

'This is Cealie,' said Tom. 'She's come with us to pick up a summer job.'

June looked mildly surprised. 'Thought you were a boy, love . . . sorry! It's the hair, I suppose. Not much in the way of high fashion down here – not used to that kind of thing. Doubt if you'll find anything at this late date; students over Swansea snap them up like locusts, see. No harm in trying, though. Welcome to stay a day or two while you're looking round . . . don't let me put you off.'

Sensing a forced politeness, I felt embarrassed. I could hear her thinking: Oh, no, not another one of Tom's lame ducks. Hope this one won't be around for long. . . .

Martin turned up – a short, stocky Welshman with dark hair and leather-brown face. Beside him, Tom seemed like a changeling, a fairy's child, with his shoulder-length brown hair and his vague manner.

'You lot can babysit for us – do something useful for a change,' he announced jovially, unbuttoning his green overalls. 'I'll take the wife down the Club. Have an evening out on the tiles for a change.'

They found me a place to sleep on the floor of the children's room.

Overheated and uncomfortable inside my sleeping bag, I lay awake for hours listening to their snufflings and their sleepy sucking sounds. They reminded me of Roz when she was very little; I could just remember. And when I finally slept, I dreamt that I was at home; that my head still lay in its nest of ringlets; that none of this had ever happened.

4

Over the next few days I tried, with an increasing sense of hopelessness, to find myself a job. Each time it was the same story. Experience? None. References? None. Previous employment? Well, a paper round. And age?

It was either things like that or the competition, which had got there before me.

'Looks just like your little brother. Never think it was a girl . . .' I overheard someone saying after one unsuccessful interview and, when I bought an ice cream, the man addressed me as 'Sonny'. So I tried out an elaborate make-up job, borrowing Martha's stuff.

The manageress of the sea-front ice-cream parlour was kind but honest. 'Quite frankly you look a bit too way out for our customers.'

You can't win, I thought wearily.

Martha and Tom began talking about moving on, hitching down to Pembroke and camping near a beach. There was obviously no place for me. Well, they had done their best, hadn't they? Taken me along with them, letting me doss down while I sorted myself out – what more could they do? Defeated and depressed, I prepared to move on, possibly even hitch-hike back to London.

'Beach'll be a nightmare today,' June said on Saturday. She was cutting sandwiches and keeping an eye on the kids who were splashing and shrieking in the blue-and-red paddling pool outside. 'Be a lot cooler up in the hills. Come with us, why don't you? See a bit of Wales before you go back to the Big Smoke. Hasn't really been much fun for you, has it? We'll go right up by the reservoir, over Tregaron way. Beautiful up there when it doesn't rain.'

'I've got a great-aunt up there.'

She's my mother's aunt, Aunt Gwennie. I remembered her from when I was very small – she was a funny old cow even then.

'Whereabouts exactly?'

'Place called Bettws.'

'Two a penny in this part of the world but we can look it up. Tregaron way, did you say it was? Why don't you pop in and say hello to her? Make her day, probably. . . .'

This crazy idea began to come together inside my head. Old Aunt Gwennie, I thought. . . . Lives by herself. A bit of a recluse. . . .

I packed up my things and brought them out to the car. 'You never know,' I joked, 'she might even ask me to stay.'

Remembering Gwennie had been pure inspiration. I knew she was still alive because we still sent her the obligatory family Christmas card. My mother never talks about her – well, why should she?

As we left the main road and began to climb I started working out a cover story. It was brilliant. You see, years ago, my mother's older sister, Nancy, emigrated to Canada. We get the annual news letter from her but there is no real contact. I could pretend

28

to be her daughter. I knew that she had one but I did not think that Gwen would have much information about her, and by the time she had sorted out the facts – if she ever got round to it – I could be long gone.

A stone cottage in the Black Mountains. . . . It sounded quite romantic, like something from a fairytale.

After the picnic the kids passed out all over us.

'Time to turn round, I suppose,' said June. 'Don't have to go straight back though. Bettws, did you say?'

We checked it out on the map.

The nearest Bettws to Tregaron turned out to be a scrubby little village in the back of nowhere.

'You don't mean old Gwennie Davies Ty Gwyn?' said the woman in the shop when I asked. The others were waiting in the car, hoping, I felt, to be shot of me.

'Ty Gwyn?'

'That's the name of her house. Daft Gwennie, we call her. No disrespect, mind you. Harmless, poor old thing. Wouldn't hurt a fly, our Gwennie. . . . You quite sure that's who you want?'

'Absolutely.'

'Some sort of relative then, are you? Someone ought to be keeping an eye on her, goodness knows. Miss Matthias is no youngster and meals on wheels a couple of times a week isn't much. Where you from then, boyo?'

I thought quickly. 'Swansea.'

'Oh yes? You don't sound Welsh.'

'My mother's English,' I said glibly.

The cottage was the only house along a short, metalled track which ended abruptly on the hillside.

29

Its once whitewashed walls were blistered and peeling and its overgrown garden ran amok around an old apple tree. The bundle of tat in gaping bedroom slippers had to be Gwennie. A couple of metal curlers dangled from her hair. When I opened the gate she looked up sharply.

'Trespassing,' she grumbled. 'Private property. . . .'

'But I'm Gail, Aunt Gwennie,' I announced cheerfully. I had forgotten my cousin's real name and thought that this had a suitably trans-Atlantic flavour. 'I am your grand-niece.' I had been working out the relationship. It was not an easy one but I thought I had it right.

'Who?'

I simplified it for her. 'Nancy's daughter . . . your niece's girl.'

You could see her chewing it over, mumbling away to herself.

'Oh yes . . .' she said vaguely. 'Very nice. . . . Come in then . . . Have a cup of tea.'

I followed her inside. The room smelt musty. She lowered herself cautiously into an armchair and settled into the cushions like a cat. I dropped my bags and perched politely on the edge of the threadbare sofa. I was trying to find something dazzling to say when she leaned forward and glared at me.

'Don't you come here with your old fibs!'

For a second I thought that she could see right through me and I began to panic. Then she said, 'They must think I'm a little bit simple, sending me a boy who tells me he's someone's daughter. No respect these days. . . .'

She said it. Not me.

Now I was really covered.

'Can I stay with you for a few days? I won't be a nuisance.'

'Please yourself. . . . Won't find much to do round Bettws.'

'But I want to spend some time with you,' I lied.

As they prepared to leave, Martha and June fussed over me. 'Sure you'll be alright?' they enquired hopefully.

I gave them the answer they needed. 'I'll be fine. Don't worry.'

We hugged self-consciously.

'Ring,' said June, 'if there are any problems. We can easily pick you up – no trouble at all.' But her relief when I waved goodbye was almost tangible.

I was amazed at how easy it had all been.

I mean, my cover story was not really so brilliant; anyone could have picked holes in it. My voice had no trace of a Canadian accent, and there was no advance warning of my arrival, not even a postcard. Yet the old lady had swallowed it whole, questioning nothing but my gender. The fact that I claimed to be 'family' seemed to be enough for her: she even went through some half-remembered guest routine, fussing about the damp and the dangers of breathing the night air.

By early evening she had given up and had put herself to bed. I was left to my own devices. I did not waste time looking for clean sheets – there probably weren't any. Instead, I dumped my stuff in a small upstairs room and went foraging for snacks. In the absence of a fridge, a half-full bottle of milk, uncovered and already smelling cheesy, had been placed on the stone flags in the corner of the pantry. Apart from a couple of eggs which could have been

31

weeks old, there seemed to be no fresh food. Finally, scrabbling through a miscellany of rusty biscuit tins, I came across an open packet of dubious digestives which hunger forced me into eating. Outside, swallows tweeted and swooped in the deepening sky. What now, I asked myself. What next? And what the hell am I doing here?

In the twilight I walked through the tangle of her garden, scrambled over the ruins of the dry stone wall and walked up to the first dark wrinkle of the hill. The grass was bleached and dry but the air was fragrant with gorse and heather and wild thyme. A rock loomed, unexpectedly white. I squatted on its smooth surface, folding my legs and trying to induce some of the calm, the detachment, which Mum is forever claiming she finds in yoga.

The feelings that came in its place were anything but peaceful.

Guilt hung round my neck like a noose. My mother had not really thrown me out – I knew that. Her 'Get out' was meant to be a temporary banishment, not a permanent one; she had said it on other occasions when she had run out of answers. Too bad, I thought: people should choose their words more carefully. She would be regretting it now. I knew how she was: she would be worried, dead scared – all those evil things she loves to quote at me from the gutter-press threatening her baby girl; her imagination working overtime. You see, I do not have to worry about myself: she does it all for me.

And my father? I did not suppose that he had been able to tear himself away from the book he was currently hooked on for long enough to notice my absence. He runs our local bookshop – largely, I suspect, to support his own addiction. We are depressingly middle class.

I wish I had been born a tramp, a gipsy, a clown. . . .

It was funny, though – ending up here.

Miss Matthias, Gwennie's social worker or whatever she is, called in today. She is also convinced of my masculinity. Why not? I am not wearing any make-up and my breasts are pretty non-existent. The woman in the shop called me 'boyo'. So be it: males have a better deal anyway.

'See you've got yourself a young man now, Gwennie.' She sounded as if she was chatting up a mentally backward five-year-old. 'There's a lucky girl you are. . . .' She turned to me. 'Your auntie's not really much with us these days, poor old soul.' Her tone had not changed in the least and she did not even lower her voice. 'What's your name then, boyo?'

I had to do some quick thinking. 'Sam.' It was the first boy's name that came into my head.

'Up here for the summer holidays, are you?'

'That's right.'

'Surprised at your parents letting you stay here alone, although she's quite harmless, poor old love. Wouldn't hurt a fly, our Gwennie, would you, love? Gentle as a little lamb . . . except when she's off preaching and that doesn't happen too often, thank goodness. Where you from then?'

I stuck to the fib I'd given them in the shop. 'Swansea,' I said glibly.

'There's nice. Had a cousin, died years ago, lived in Swansea. . . . Well, if you have any problems with her just come over and knock on my door. You here for long?'

'A couple of weeks.'

'Mam coming to fetch you?'

I did not disagree.

'Not much for a youngster like you to do in Bettws. Care for riding?'

'A bit.'

'Well, there's always Jinnie Evans's ponies . . . trekking . . . up on the hills, out in all weathers, wouldn't be my cup of tea. Her eldest is about your age, too.'

I privately told Jinnie Evans where to put both ponies and eldest.

'Auntie told you about her angel yet?'

'Angel?'

'No? Treat in store for you, then. Sees an angel up in her old apple tree, love her – don't you, Gwen?'

'Don't I what?' Gwennie had had enough of her and, frankly, so had I.

'I was telling Sam here about your angel.'

'Go home and mind your own business, Doris Matthias. No angels round here.'

'I'm just going. . . .' She leaned towards me, her breath smelling of sweet tea. 'Don't you take any silly nonsense from her now.'

It had been raining since early morning, but now patches of brightness had blossomed between the clouds. I had already been down to the shop for a few basics – cornflakes, sliced bread, packets of ham and cheese, fresh biscuits and coffee and some long-life milk.

Gwennie was dozing again. I decided to make myself some sandwiches and go out for a long walk.

Confined to a house I get wriggly and irritable. It felt so good to stride out across the sodden heather, that rich, undulating countryside all mine, shared only by the straying herds of wild ponies and a few browsing sheep. Whenever the sun shone – briefly – the earth steamed.

I kept seeing frogs, almost stepping on them sometimes. They are good to tease with grass stems but difficult to catch. Once I managed to pick one up and hold it, pulsing with terror, in the palm of my hand. Its back was like a freckled yellow leaf and its eyes glinted and flickered like shiny little beads. I like frogs; I do not understand how people can be squeamish about them.

Daft as a little kid, I leapt over the hedgehog clumps of reeds. My feet sank into rich, yielding carpets of acid-green moss full of brown peat bubbles but I did not give a damn. There was a stream at the bottom of the hill, tawny and bright, spreading out its stony beach of terracotta pink like a comet's tail, and I soaked off the mud in its clear water. When the rain came again in a fine, pinprick spray, I waded downstream to shelter under the bridge. My shoes and the legs of my jeans were already drenched but I did not fancy soggy sandwiches.

When I got back I stuffed my shoes full of old newspapers and turned them upside-down to dry. Gwen, awake now, watched me scornfully.

'Call those shoes?' They were once pink-and-white trainers. 'More like my bedroom slippers. Mam needs her head read. . . .'

'They're running shoes: lots of people wear them.'

'Lots of silly fools then. . . .'

'Well, I don't have any others.'

35

She tottered over to the larder, fumbled about in the darkness and emerged with a pair of battered leather boots that looked like something from a museum. Her fingers were trembling.

'Proper boots, these are . . . your Uncle John's . . . made to last, not like that old rubbish. Put them on.'

I will try anything once.

I giggled. 'They'll never fit me.' But I was wrong.

'Had very small feet for a man, your uncle. . . .'

I have very large ones for a girl. They have been a problem ever since I can remember. These archaeological specimens felt like iron, but, unbelievably, they did seem to be the right size.

'Uncle John your husband?'

'Love you, no. Brother. Never had no husband. Old maid, see. Haven't missed much, from what I hear. . . .'

Listen. My Aunt Gwennie has this thin, straight-across mouth as sensible as the boots she had just lent me and about as sexy. She is short, cushiony at the rump and her scant hair is a sort of tobacco-stained white and wound in places around these little metal curlers which she mostly forgets to remove. She even has a moustache. For a moment I tried to imagine her young and sexy, fancying a bloke – but I could not do it.

I mean, I cannot even think of my own mother in those terms.

But I did wonder about the angel.

I looked at her again. What kind of a dream lay drowned in those watery blue eyes?

5

My conscience has got the better of me: I have rung Roz. It was hell.

There is only one public telephone in Bettws and it does not work. No, it has not been vandalized, as it might have been at home, but, like my aunt, it seems to be confused: the receiver clicks and babbles; you hear strange snatches of conversation, and then it seems to go to sleep. Someone is supposed to be coming over to look at it. Tomorrow, maybe. Perhaps the day after that. Possibly never. In the meantime my parents might have been bleating to the police about my disappearance. I had to stop them, re-assure them, tell them that everything is under control, shut them up.

The shop had a telephone. I hated asking for favours but I had no choice.

The village shop is not much bigger than our bathroom and it smells of over-ripe apples and stale newspapers. One bit of it is trying to be a super-market but they still keep most things behind the counter. The bleak post-office section attracts docile queues. The couple who run the place work at their own snail's pace, pausing frequently for a chat.

'Run off my feet today. . . .' The familiar woman

with the fluffed-out red hair addressed the world at large. At her plump armpits, her pink terylene blouse was stained damp.

'Could I possibly use your phone?'

'Oh, not another one. . . . Been like this all morning and yesterday too. Diawl, but I'll be thankful when they fix that thing. Go on then; give me your ten p, and make it short. Presume it's local; better be. . . .'

'I've got to ring someone in London.'

'Oh no, boyo, no question of it.'

'Oh please . . . it's really urgent. I can pay you for it – look.'

There is money stashed away all over that house. Gwennie's got no use for it.

'Not even if it's a matter of life or death.'

'Oh please . . . it's very urgent and there's nowhere else to ring from.'

'Everything alright up at Ty Gwyn?'

'Oh yes.'

'Nothing wrong with our Gwennie, then?'

'She's fine. Please?'

'Come on then – Sam they call you, is it? Just this once then. I must be going soft in the head. It's over there.'

'Hello . . . Person to person, yes, that's right . . . Rosamund Thomson. Roz, is that you?'

'. . . they'll be ringing New York next . . .'

'Cealie! Where are you? Are you alright?'

'I'm fine.'

'We've all been going out of our minds. Mum! I've got Cealie!'

'I don't want to speak to her,' I said quickly.

'Why not?'

'She threw me out, didn't she?'

38

'Cealie, that's not fair! You know she didn't mean it . . . she wouldn't. She was just upset about you going and getting all your hair cut off. What's it look like now? Can't wait to see you punk—'

'Tell her I'm OK.'

'So, when are you coming home?'

'I don't know. Not yet . . . maybe never. . . .'

'You can't say that.'

'Why not?'

'Mum wants to know if there's a boy, a bloke.'

'Tell her no.'

'What are you doing about money?'

'There's no problem.'

'Have you got a job then?'

I hedged. 'Sort of. . . .'

'Look – Mum's in a terrible state, and even Dad's walking around looking ill the whole time. Don't you care?'

Yes, of course I did, but that was emotional blackmail. 'This is costing me a bomb – I must go.'

'They've reported you missing; there'll be trouble when they find you.' I could hear the weepy desperation in her voice.

'I'll be in touch,' I said awkwardly.

'Cealie!'

When I heard Mum's voice, I put down the telephone. At that moment she was too much inside me, with her mother-smell and her vague blue eyes and her wide, conciliatory smile. She always smiles with her mouth wide open but then her eyes often skim past you as if you are not really there, as if she is really looking for someone else. She is quite good-looking in an old sort of way. Her hair is fine and dead straight; my curls come from my dad. She used to be

39

a blonde, but now she is slowly turning a sort of transparent silver, like yellowing glass fibre. For as long as I can remember she has worn her hair caught back with one of those ornate, old-fashioned hair slides which never stays put, and around her neck she likes to wear fine chains, threads of gold or silver. I can still remember the silver filigree butterfly which hung from one of them, which I used to play with when I was very little. . . .

So that was that. I have done my duty.

Being a boy is a great disguise: no one will be looking for a boy.

My image is not completely foolproof, though. This morning the travelling butcher called me 'love' and boys are never addressed with such casual intimacy. I bought us some lamb chops. Why not? The mint in the garden must be knee-high and it is silly not to use it. I brought back a bag of potatoes and started a late lunch.

Gwennie fluttered around, 'helping', dabbing ineffectually at yesterday's dirty tea-cups and giving me odd looks from time to time. Something was obviously bothering her. At last she came out with it.

'There's funny seeing a boy cooking . . . not natural.'

I exaggerated in order to provoke her.

'At home I do it all the time.'

She frowned.

'Your mam trying to make a sissy out of you, then?'

'Why shouldn't a boy know how to cook?' I was enjoying this.

'Shouldn't have to with women around. My brother never had to boil an egg for himself . . .

40

waited on him hand and foot . . .' she was bragging now '. . . and don't regret one minute of it.'

'Was there something wrong with him?' I asked innocently.

'Wrong? What do you mean, wrong?' She was indignant. 'He was a fine man, your Uncle John. Lot of ill-health towards the end, mind you.'

'Was he very stupid then?' I was relentless.

'Stupid?' Her blood was really up now. 'What you mean, stupid?'

'A bit – feeble-minded . . . you know . . . I mean, if he couldn't even boil an egg.'

She bristled.

'You mind what you say, young man, or I'll send you packing!'

Lamb chops and mashed potatoes with a jugful of mint sauce is no meal for high summer. At home, in weather like this, we would have had salads – ice-cold cucumber, green and red peppers and fat little spring onions. Here they do not go much for fresh vegetables; the only lettuces I have seen have been small and scrubby and limp as shrivelled silk. 'Not much call for them, see,' explains the shop lady.

I can only spend so much time in that house and then I have to get out. Listen: she has this habit of holding her fingers, coy as a fan, in front of her mouth to cover the fact that she is digging out bits of food from behind her dentures – ugh! Age is revolting. I am going to die romantically at forty. And even with all the windows open – and what a struggle it was to do that – the place smells stale.

Fat and overfed, I stumble across the moor.

I have found myself a hollow in the scoop of the hill, a real fairy dell, all thyme and heather and

41

smelling of roasting blueberries. The sun is still not low enough to make a hill shadow and it is wonderfully warm.

I pretend I am on a French beach and strip down to my knickers – might as well get myself a suntan. The thought of French beaches rings an uncomfortable bell: I remember that they booked a cottage in Brittany for sometime in August. What shall I do? Do I want to go with them? No, I do not. Look, this is real. For the first time in my life my days have no structure – I just live. And meals do not happen at mealtimes – I just eat when I'm hungry. I am by myself. I am running the whole show single-handed and I am not doing too badly. . . .

Yes, I am using some of Gwennie's pension money. No, it is not stealing. How can it be when she is not even aware of its existence? We have to eat, after all. Bet she's eating properly now for the first time in years, even if it does happen at funny hours of the day. Yesterday they brought her one of those Meals on Wheels but it didn't look very appetizing. I like cooking.

London . . . four hours away on the motorway and nothing to do with me.

I sleep late here. Gwennie doesn't notice; we don't make rules for each other.

This morning, for example, I woke up at dawn and went outside just for the pleasure of it. The hillside was all pearly and as I ran the dew pressed out, like a pale wine, between my toes. Ever seen a sunrise in the Black Mountains? It's quite something.

And I have proper bedclothes now. The sleeping bag was much too stuffy and, rummaging through Gwennie's drawers, I found some clean sheets –

laundered and folded amid a magpie's nest of twisted stockings and scarves, long-forgotten Christmas cards, old magazines and lace-edged handkerchieves with embroidered initials. Spread out, they are parchment thin and patched with tiny, delicate stitches; they smell of starch and mothballs. Once she could sew, and sew beautifully; once she was a really fine craftswoman. I have talked her into showing me some of her work – limp blouses in washed-out colours, their yokes a lattice of little stitches, and handmade lace cloths to protect the backs of her chairs – not that any rough male with slicked-back hair ever stained her flowered chintz.

Did they do all that stuff to keep their minds off sex?

I have changed her bed for her – a stinking heap – and given her fresh sheets too. Miss Matthias has taken the old ones off to be washed. She thinks I am a treasure.

'She'll be lost without you when you go. Never met a boy like you for housekeeping.'

She never met a boy like me. Period.

Oh, I am not so bad.

In a few days' time I will have another go at Roz; perhaps she will understand. . . .

Roz is just twelve and everybody's darling. She has charm in dollops. She has charisma. She even has ambition. Already she is flirting with the idea of Art School – her only problem, at present, being which one. I have no such commitment. At fifteen, quite frankly, I haven't a clue.

And she has this thing about clothes. . . .

For instance, take those arty, slightly off-beat things Mum sometimes makes for us. Like the patchwork jacket she made for my thirteenth birthday, a wondrous affair in hundreds of little diamonds of coloured silk, softly quilted, a real work of art but something I would have preferred to have put on my wall, not my back. She had been cooking it up for weeks – it was her Big Secret. How could I tell her that in it, with my lavish ringlets, I looked like a Drag Queen? She would have been so hurt if I had not worn it to the School Concert – so there I stood, done up like the Christmas Fairy, trying to ignore the nudges and innuendoes, concentrating grimly on my music. 'A Coat of Many Colours,' my art teacher had gushed, and it had taken me at least six months to live that one down.

Now when Roz inherited that jacket, things were quite different. She is a different shape from me: I mean, at eleven it fitted her perfectly. Her friends went ga-ga: 'It's amazing.' 'Is it very old?' 'Wherever did you find it?' 'Your *mother*? Aren't you *lucky*?'

Well, schools are different. Attitudes change. I wish, though, that some of the good things had come my way. Even her hair – she has hair like Mum's, straight and fine, the sort you can cut really well. She wears it short, of course; there is nothing twee about my little sister.

Yes, of course I am envious, but it doesn't stop me liking her. The charm works on me, too.

A straggle of riders is moving across the horizon. Damn! I pull on my shirt in case they come close. This thing about horses – I never had it. I would rather drive a car.

They are swerving and veering this way. The little figures grow large. I am irritated. I do not welcome this grubby bunch of strangers, laughing and calling

44

out to each other, disgustingly jolly. Squatting here in the heather, I feel very conspicuous, so I get up and fake interest in a nearby rock.

The boy out in front has one of the ponies by the rein; its rider looks sullen and cross.

'Hullo,' he says, glancing down at me in a superior sort of way. His fair, straggly hair is lank with sweat.

I say: 'Hi!' and go on studying my rock. In this situation, my sister Roz would have been studying him. I wonder, vaguely, which sex he thinks I am, and whether he would have spoken at all if he had thought that I was a boy. Or perhaps it was the other way round. This odd situation has made me suddenly aware of these fine points of human behaviour which I had scarcely noticed before.

Moving off, the swinging backsides of the ponies and the crumbs of dry turf spat out by their heels fill my whole field of vision, larger than life. I am relieved when they become part of the landscape again, just moving brown shapes against greys and pinks and greens.

You see, I like my solitude.

6

Last night I took my sleeping bag out on to the hillside and slept under the stars.

It was scary, walking out into that grey and silver world; like being in a strange room at night, with nothing familiar, nothing you can name. Black humps were clearly rocks until, shifting, they began cropping the moon-bleached grass. Each bush, each clump of reeds could have been a monster and everything moving was suspect until I could identify it.

On the dampening grass I lay, wrapped in my warm cocoon, listening to the little sounds of the night. When I held out my fingers they were bright like glow-worms; the inky sky was rich with stars – I had never seen so many. I thought about all those other worlds up there, all those planets and faraway suns, and it made me feel very small and alone. This was how it must have been at the beginning, I thought. Then people tried to reduce it all into terms which they could understand, in the way that Mum makes everything into her own kind of prettiness.

I slept through a sunrise and my eyes flipped open to a high blue sky where a tissue-paper moon still lingered. At first I thought that the roof had blown away in the night. Then my fingers met the damp, prickly pelt of the hill and I remembered where I was.

I wriggled out of my sleeping bag and went off to pee behind a modesty screen of ferns. Half-asleep still, I wet my foot but it did not bother me in the least; the damp turf would soon wipe it clean. A spider had hung a small, glittering web over one of Uncle John's boots. Earth-scented, exhilarated, I felt as if I had been living this way for weeks. If the weather kept up, perhaps I could. The only problem would be food.

The thought of food immediately conjured up seductive pictures of bread and jam and hot tea. I rolled up the sleeping bag, laced up the incredible boots and scrambled back down to the cottage.

The front door was wide open, which was odd, as Gwen does not usually wake up until well past noon. I wondered if I had been careless, yet I was certain I had closed it properly; my mother fusses so much about security that locking doors is second nature to me. The cottage looks so tatty who would bother to burgle it? It might be tempting as a squat, though – I may not be the only tramp around here. It was an uncomfortable thought.

Worried, I ran upstairs. I know my rights and I got here first. Anyway she is my aunt.

'Auntie Gwennie!' I shouted.

The bed was empty. Twisted sheets and blankets, a pink elastic stocking and – God knows why – a ragged tea-towel marked out the hollow in which she had been lying. Like a good detective I touched it and found it cold. She had left, then, quite some time ago.

I panicked and ran all over the place, calling out and opening doors. I checked the sitting room again but clearly she was not there. In the deserted kitchen I tried the pantry. Some half-remembered ghoulish tale about an old woman who had died locked inside her own lavatory sent me running even there, flinging the door against the pock-marked wall in a shower of flaked whitewash, but the curved wooden seat stood empty as an abandoned throne and the blackened metal chain hung like a plumbline.

I ran back across the garden and out on to the hill, aware that it was a waste of time for the hills did not seem to interest her and she could never have ventured so far. I tried the road, running down to the junction and waving at a passing van; the driver, if he noticed me at all, must have taken me for the village idiot, for he did not attempt to stop.

I was frightened. I was afraid of finding her and afraid of not finding her. Perhaps I was flapping over nothing. Maybe she did sometimes take herself out for a walk and why not? She was still able to walk with a stick, wasn't she?

Remembering my gran who would never step out of doors without a hat and coat, I riffled through her assortment of clothes – a smelly fur thing showing the white of its skin, a couple of crimplene horrors and a plastic mac – and her Oxfam collection of fancy hats, but how was I to know? Suddenly I thought of her handbag, that hideous, overstuffed brown leather pouch from which she was never separated. There was no sign of it. I turned over cushions, looked inside, behind and under things. It was not there.

Forcing myself out of panic I made a pot of tea and buttered some slices of bread. She would turn up. She was bound to turn up at some time. Wouldn't she?

But supposing she did not? Then the police would

come and expose my pathetic little lies and track down my family and I would be accused of God knows what. I tried to eat but my appetite had all gone.

And supposing there had been an accident? I mean, what would I do if I found her, all mangled and twisted, in some unlikely place? Me? Pretty little Cecilia who has never had to deal with a real emergency in her life? Move her? But that might make things much worse. Run down to the village for help and come back and find her dead?

In the warm sun, the butter was fast becoming a yellow slime. I put the dish back on to the flagstones to cool and threw the bread in the dustbin.

I was hanging my sleeping bag over the apple tree to air – I had to do something – when a car pulled up outside. My stomach instantly contracted. This is it, I thought.

Then Miss Matthias came round and started fussing over the passenger door. Out staggered Gwen, dressed to kill and looking very pleased with herself. A pink woolly coat half-covered her long flowered night-dress which was mud-splashed and torn in several places. Thick, coffee-coloured stockings wrinkled into brown leather lace-ups and a pale blue feathered hat hung askew over one eye. With her stick wildly waving, she was just like a drunken queen. I began to wonder if she was. Drunk, I mean. There was this sort of shiny-eyed, ecstatic look about her.

'Oh, she's been a naughty girl,' Miss Matthias clucked brightly. 'Worried the life out of your little boyfriend, you have. Look at his face. Been out preaching again, haven't you, lovey? Sam will make you a nice cup of tea. Sit down here . . . all over now till the next time. Didn't they tell you, then?' she added when I did not move. 'Then – how were they to know? Never come here to see her themselves, do they?'

'What should they have told me?'

'Only that Auntie sometimes takes herself off on these little jaunts. . . . Blame myself for not mentioning it sooner. Been doing it for donkey's years now, haven't you, Gwen? Likes all the fuss she causes, I think, and the little ride back in someone's car.'

'When the Lord calls me, I'm always ready to go.' The unexpected assurance of this statement was mocked by the silly hat. 'I've done my duty. Now I'd like a nice cup of tea.'

I went into the kitchen and filled the kettle. I needed one myself. When I got back, she was already asleep, slumped against the wing of the armchair, her face all squashy, her mouth open, and the blue hat perched on her shoulder like Long John Silver's parrot.

'Sleeping it off,' sniffed Miss Matthias. 'She'll be out like a light until tomorrow. Better get her upstairs and tucked in. Gwen!' She shook the old woman's shoulder. 'Sam's brought you some tea!'

Now it was all over, I was curious. Up till now I had found her slow, confused, funny sometimes, sometimes quite acid, but not daft, not barmy – just an old woman and a bit muddled. Now she seemed to be on a private hotline to God, as well as keeping an angel as a pet. I was fascinated.

'How does the Lord call you?' It was a real question, not a tease.

'She sees her angel, love her, don't you, Gwen?'

I snapped.

'I asked Auntie Gwen, not you.' I hope that there is no one like Miss Matthias around me when I am old.

'I'm chosen, you see,' Gwen explained modestly. 'Like Mary.' Not in quite the same way though, I thought. 'The angel always tells me what to do. "Bring the Word to Bettws," he says, and I do.'

'What does he look like?'

'You know what angels look like, Boyo, no need to ask me that. White all over and wings growing out of his back. . . .' She sighed. 'Beautiful he is. . . .'

I noticed with amusement that this angel of hers was male. A bloke. Gabriel, I supposed. She was a virgin after all. . . .

My mother thinks that I am still a virgin. Well, we all have our little fantasies. . . . Sometimes I believe that she is still a virgin, that perhaps she really did find us under cabbages or rose bushes – prettier that way.

Sex is over-rated anyway.

I performed the great act at a party, actually. I did it so that I could be like the rest of them, not because I really wanted to. Everyone I know except Ranjit has had some sexual experience. I expected something ecstatic. It just hurt. Masturbation is much more satisfying. Do I hear you saying something like: 'Ah but you have never been in love?' You are dead right. I did not even fancy him. I was curious, wanting to know what all the fuss was about. It was a drag.

You see, for weeks afterwards I was obsessed by the possibility that I might be pregnant. The fantasy of a living person growing inside me all because of an uncomfortable ten minutes behind the coat pile was like something out of science fiction. It was a silly risk to take – he didn't even use a condom – but I did need to know. It would be so nice to be able to do the right thing at the right time, but life isn't like that. Life isn't pretty – it's a mess. And love is all dirtied up with hurting.

I mean – look what I'm doing to my family. . . .

Thoughts like this scuttled around inside my head, nagging at me, biting me and driving me eventually down to the village to ring Roz again.

When she came to the telephone her voice was tight and unnatural. She knew who was calling.

'Cealie?' Sometimes we are almost telepathic.

'Roz. Look, I'm just ringing to let you know that I'm still OK.' I felt stiff and self-conscious.

'Do you want to speak to Mum?'

'Look I can't—'

'Dad then—'

'No.'

'Then I don't really think I want to talk to you.'

'Look, Roz—' In an odd sort of way, I needed her. I needed her quite desperately.

They have fixed the public telephone at last. I was grateful for that when the line went dead and I burst into tears.

Inside the shop, where I had gone to get myself a comfort bar of chocolate, I found the pony-trekking bloke buying stamps. He recognized me at once.

'You the kid who's staying up at Gwennie Davies's?'

'That's right,' I said nonchalantly, hoping that the tears had evaporated.

'There's a fuss your old auntie made down here yesterday.'

'Really?' I wanted to sound non-committal but it had no effect on this guy.

'Really, yes, really. We never thought she'd lay on one of her performances with a guest in the house, though.'

I was irritated but curious. What exactly had she been up to?

'What was she actually doing?' I asked reluctantly.

'You mean you don't know?'

'Not much. Miss Matthias said something about her preaching. . . .'

'Preaching – you can say that again!' The red-haired woman had picked up the theme with enthusiasm and now there was no stopping her. 'Comes tottering down the street on her stick – Lord knows where she finds the strength, they say she's almost bed-ridden most of the time. Comes toddling along, dressed up to the nines, hat and all, parks herself right next to that big angel in the graveyard next to Ebenezer Chapel and starts yacking away nineteen to the dozen about hellfire, heaven's harps, Jesu's little lambs . . . you name it. Kids give her a hard time if they spot her . . . Daft Gwennie . . . she's a bit of a local joke, see, poor old soul. Ought to be in a home if you ask me, no offence meant, mind.'

If we had not left when we did she would have gone on all day.

'Old Matthias told me you were Sam. I'm Glyn – Glyn Evans. She's quite worked up about you, you know. Says you can't put an old head on young shoulders and the strain is beginning to show – told Mam you nearly bit her head off this morning.'

God, is nothing private in Bettws?

'Well, I was worried.'

We walked on in silence.

'Surprised they let you stay there by yourself,' he said at last.

'And who are these mysterious "they"?' I asked crossly.

'Your family, I suppose. Aren't they a bit concerned?'

I was annoyed but I had to be careful.

'Not really . . . I mean, they know she's a bit potty but she's quite harmless,' I opened up my chocolate bar. 'We don't visit her regularly, of course – much too far.'

That was a mistake.

'Swansea's not so far.' He sounded almost accusing. 'And suppose something happened?'

'Like what?'

'She could get ill, fall down, wander off in the wrong direction and end up under a car.'

'I can cope,' I said stiffly. I was suddenly aware of my 'boy' act and started working at it, deliberately stepping heavily and swinging my shoulders in a manner I hoped was aggressive.

'She can't be your auntie,' he said after a while. 'She's too old, man.' If I can fool him, I thought delightedly, I can fool anybody.

'Actually she's my great-aunt,' I said, my confidence returning. 'My gran's sister, not my mother's.'

'Want to come out trekking one afternoon?'

'Can't afford it.'

'You wouldn't have to pay anything. Miss Matthias told me to ask you. Said it wasn't healthy for you up there all by yourself.'

I was cross: 'I wish she'd mind her own business.'

'Her way of caring, I suppose. She's not a bad old thing, just clumsy . . . supposed to have a heart of

54

gold if you dig for it. Come out anyway; I wouldn't mind having a bit of help apart from my brother. Some of those kids don't know one end of a horse from the other.'

'And what gives you the idea that I'm any better?'

He grinned at me. His hair was damp from the rain and his face was pink and freckled and sort of innocent. Not my type. Not my type at all.

'You seem pretty sensible to me,' he said. 'Some of them get so steamed up watching the girls' arses they'd ride straight over a precipice if someone didn't keep an eye on them.'

I grinned. No problems there.

'Ridden before, have you?'

'A bit.' I thought of my half-dozen riding lessons of a few years back, churning up the mud in Trent Park, and suddenly saw myself galloping across the heather like a great romantic hero. Or heroine.

The temptation was just too great.

'Alright,' I said. 'Thanks.'

7

What the hell am I doing here?

Early evening, and dirty pillows of cloud smother the hills and hang, dripping, above the leaf-lattice of apple and elder, rowen and hawthorn. I am damp and disillusioned and I would sell my soul for a hot bath. After the long ride, my legs are stiff and sore and the underneath of my chin itches from the strap of the borrowed riding hat which Glyn insisted on: evidently a conventional type who never breaks the rules. Romantic? You must be joking. It was simply painful and wet and there wasn't even a view: the thick cloud veiled distance and smudged everything closer into pastel.

Gwen is drowsing over a mug of warm milk. Boredom rules OK. I have switched on the room's only light – a rosebowl of dead flies suspended by three rusty chains from the ceiling. There are faded pink squiggles on the wallpaper which might once have been flowers. A seaweed stain of mould grows round the gold-framed photograph of my grand-mother's wedding. Beneath the waxen blossoms and the white lace of the veil her eyes seem dark and frightened, like those of a cornered animal. Gwennie, the only bridesmaid, displays her posy like a freshly-picked cabbage.

In the morning Glyn drops by to ask me over for supper and a video. Some of the trekkers stay at the house, so one more or less, he tells me, makes no difference.

I think Gwen is quite jealous.

'You don't want,' she says, 'to go running round too much with the boys from the village.'

I am amused.

'Why ever not?'

She is vague.

'Bit rough, some of them. Keep yourself to yourself, that's my policy.' Unexpectedly she asks coyly: 'You got a little sweetheart?' She answers that one for herself. 'No . . . bit too young for all that silly nonsense.'

'Did you,' I ask artfully, 'ever have a sweetheart, Auntie Gwen?'

I enjoy teasing her a little, drawing her out: I mean, she does have a past. At the back of a cupboard stuffed full of the most unbelievable junk, I have unearthed an album. The gold-embossed flower spray on its damp blue cover is spotted white and stinks of mildew but the cards and photographs inside are quite fascinating. Here she is, a stiff, unbending young woman with a tight, self-conscious smile, her eyes pools of melancholy under the piled-up hair, but really not bad-looking, not bad-looking at all. But when I show it to her she frowns and blinks through her spectacles and says, 'Wonder I didn't break the camera.' How many times in her life has she said that, I wondered.

Perhaps Gran was the pretty one. . . .

'I had my young men like everyone else,' she sniffs. 'Had more important things to do, see.'

'What kind of things?'

'Who'd you think was going to look after Mam after Dada went? And then John never did marry . . . no one to care for him and it's not good for a man to be on his own. Helpless as little babies, love them, without a woman round the house. Gone now, John. . . .' She is silent, still grieving. I do not know what to say.

'Don't you get mixed up with Megan, now.' With one of her illogical leaps she has gone sideways, leaving me baffled. Megan?

'Why shouldn't I?' I will go along with this Megan story and see what comes out.

'Flighty little piece, my sister, though blood's thicker than water and I shouldn't say it . . .' Her fingers play nervously with a grubby lace handkerchief. '. . . and her youngest – now there's a handful for you . . . chip off the old block. . . .'

I suddenly realize that I am irretrievably mixed up with this Megan woman because of course she is my grandmother. And her youngest? There are possibilities in this.

'A flighty girl, your Auntie Winnie. . . .'

At first I have no idea who she is talking about.

'Winnie?'

Once again I am someone of her own generation, a village gossip.

'That girl will come to no good in the end, I keep telling you.'

The past and the present are all on the same level for Gwen. 'Nice little thing, though . . . used to come up here a lot once. . . . Mind you, I gave help when help was needed, didn't I? She's my niece after all, my own flesh and blood. . . .'

58

Her niece. Something goes click inside my head.

'Who was Winnie's sister? What was she called?' I have to check out my theory.

'Nancy, of course, you silly boy.'

Winnie? Oh, this is a good one.

My mother has even invented herself.

You see, I thought her Christian name was Freda; I mean – even Gran had been trained to call her that. Freda. It sounds Scandinavian, doesn't it? And it goes so well with her long fair hair and her grey-blue eyes – she must have known that. It is short for Winifred, but she has never used her full name. Had she, one day, said: call me Freda from now on? Was anything about her real? I feel frightened without knowing why.

Why shouldn't she have changed her name? I have become Cealie, after all, and if she had called me Winnie I would most certainly have done something about it.

Names are like wrapping paper.

'Winnie' is a nasty cardboard-brown and printed all over with horses' heads: I would not care to be a Winnie.

But then 'Cecilia' is prayer-book pure and much too precious to be used at all. And as for 'Rosamund' . . . that is all tissue-paper roses; no wonder she shortened it to Roz. Myself, I like 'Sam': it is sailor-jolly, tough and practical. Gift-wrapped as 'Sam' I feel ready for anything.

'Why did Winnie need your help?' I am curious.

At this point, in comes Miss Matthias, cheerful as chintz, spoiling it all, marching over our egg-shell intimacy in her sensible brown leather sandals.

'Afternoon, Gwen – just popping in. There's a

lovely day it is, a change from yesterday. See you've still got your young man.'

'I like to have a man about the house,' says Gwen smugly.

Miss Matthias is amused by this.

'Seems to me this one's a bit undersized – needs to put on a bit of muscle. And he won't be here for ever, Gwen – don't go getting that idea in your head. When will you be going home, Sam?'

Is she trying to throw me out?

'In a couple of weeks, I suppose.'

'Then you'll be all by yourself again, Gwen. Lost without him, you'll be.'

This is clearly ridiculous: I have only been here for just over a week and I am not indispensable. She is up to something. . . .

'Not very nice being on your own again . . . suppose you fell? Had a little accident? These things can happen. Better to be somewhere snug where you can be properly looked after.' She turns to me. 'I keep telling your Auntie but she'll never listen.'

Perhaps we should both run away and join a commune, Gwen and I.

'Trying to get me into the Workhouse again—'

'Workhouse? Nonsense. You know better than that, Gwennie Davies. All mod. cons., central heating, a telly to watch and lots of friendly people to chat to.' Aside, to me, she adds quietly: 'Vacancy's just come up and she really ought to take it before she gets any worse. It's the isolation that does it, I'm sure. Losing her marbles she is, poor love . . . those silly preaching bouts and the kids can be so cruel . . . they don't understand.'

I lose my patience with her.

60

'You are the one who doesn't understand! She doesn't want to go – can't you see?'

'Oh, so you'll stay here and look after her, then.' I am shattered by her fierceness. 'Why don't your lot come up and do something about her then instead of sending a kid up here to sponge on her and get a cheap holiday into the bargain!'

When she sees my reaction she is suddenly penitent.

'Oh, I'm sorry. I shouldn't have said that, let my tongue run away with me.' She is scratching words over the hurt like a dog burying its turd. 'I didn't mean to upset you like that – look, I've said I'm sorry, haven't I?' Then she suddenly gets it together. 'But a lot of old nonsense is spouted by people like you who've ducked out of the situation themselves. I've no patience with it . . . and dying alone can be slow and painful and not very pretty at all.'

Chastened, I have no reply.

For all her fussiness and lack of finesse, this woman is strong, solid. It does not make me like her any more but she does have my respect.

'Swansea you're from, is it? Not the moon and back, is it?'

Remembering the 'Canada' story I had fed to Gwen, I am troubled. Living a lie is exhausting. Nothing fits properly. I am almost tempted to reveal all, to bare my undersized breasts and shock her – but would she be shocked? An hour ago I would have said yes: she would scream and fall about. Now I am no longer sure. I am no longer sure about anything and I need someone. You? Oh, you are just a thought bubble, a skinful of air, and Roz will not listen any more. Someone. Who?

61

Ranjit is a possibility. I know her number. I might get her brother or one of her parents but the risk is worth it for a few minutes of being me, myself, Cealie.

I walk down to the village and dial the code. The voice – not hers – is vaguely familiar.

'Could I speak to Ranjit, please?'

'Cealie!'

My God, it is my mother! While I was working out what to say, my fingers, like performing dogs, have gone through their automatic routine of dialling home.

'Cealie, where are you?'

I can hear the desperation and the hurt. I consider opting out. Replacing the receiver would be such a simple mechanical act, but I cannot do it.

'Hullo, Mum.' What can I say to her?

'I'm going out of my mind with worry. Why won't you speak to me?'

That one is easy.

'Why should I? You threw me out, didn't you?'

'I don't know what you're talking about – threw you out? You know very well I would never do such a thing. Are you crazy?'

' "Get out" is what you said.'

'Out of my sight, temporarily – yes. But I've said that to you before. How could you possibly think. . . ?'

'Well, I did.' My voice is curt. I am aware of hurting. I need to hurt; I do not know why. 'In future you should be more careful.' Why is cruelty so enjoyable? I know I am going to feel pretty terrible about this but right now, at this moment, I feel like a ruthless warrior cutting through her weakness with my cold, glittering blade.

There is a shocked silence. Then: 'Are you on drugs?'

Oh, it cannot be her sweet Cecilia who never gets angry. . . .

'I don't think so.'

'Look.' Her voice is thick with tears. 'I'm sorry if I hurt you; I didn't mean to. Please come home from wherever you are – where are you, Cealie?'

My throat is beginning to ache. 'A very long way from London.'

Irritatingly I too seem to want to cry and it clouds my thinking.

'Where?' She is almost hysterical.

'I can't tell you.' I will not be undermined in this way. 'Look, I'm alright. Hasn't Roz told you that? Isn't that enough for you?'

'We've cancelled the cottage—'

'Oh Christ, because of me? Look, can't you understand? I'm a person in my own right. I'm almost sixteen. I need to work things out. Can't you trust me?'

'Did you really expect us to go away for jolly hols not knowing where you were or what was happening to you?'

My tolerance is rapidly running out – why won't she listen?

'I've given you my word that I'm alright. Do you have to know the details?'

'So just when do you propose coming home?' Her voice has hardened. Good. This I can deal with but spare me the tears – they make me feel so guilty.

'I can't say. I'll keep in touch though.'

'Don't say that. Don't speak to me like that, as if I were some casual acquaintance or a total stranger.'

63

'Perhaps in some respects you are.' Gwen's random comments are still lying undigested inside me . . . a handful, Winnie . . . chip off the old block . . . gave help when help was needed. . . . 'Mum,' I ask unguardedly, 'were you a difficult teenager?'

The pips begin to go.

'Give me your number and I'll ring back.'

Give her this number? She must be joking! Subtle stuff, though: gets me talking and then tries to pull a fast one. Give her this number? Not on your nellie. I put down the phone.

My head is all choked up with anger now. I am furious with her. Listen. Some girls move in with boyfriends. Some girls live in squats. Some girls go on the hard stuff or simply drop out of sight. Me – I go off by myself for the first time in my life, ring them several times to reassure them, like a good little girlie, but will they take my word for it? No they will not. To them I am still a dependent child, accountable for all my actions to adults whose own lives do not, quite frankly, impress me.

Take my dad. What does he know about the real world? He just lives with his favourite toys, like an overgrown baby in a playpen.

My anger comes back with me to the cottage and I am restless and snappy with Gwen. She is family too and basically the same thing. I mean, if she were not so confused she would probably think she had the right to tell me what to think and what to do and what to feel.

I used to like Dad's shop. I used to feel quite proud of working there, helping out on Saturday afternoons and the occasional school holiday. Once I really enjoyed those times, kidding myself that I was really close to this quiet, solitary person with his off-beat, gentle sense of humour which could bite but rarely damage. Not many people were allowed into his private world. I used to think that I was. I know better now.

There were these people in my class who began talking about something called elitism.

'Who's your bloody bookshop for?' they would ask. 'Who are your dad's customers? People just like you.'

And I used to defend him, telling them about the children's room where the books are put out on little tables for the kids to browse through and Mum does storytelling sessions dressed up all sparkly, but it made no difference.

Then one day I understood.

The shoplifter was one of the girls in my class. She was not a friend exactly, but I knew quite a bit about her. Sandra didn't have a dad and her mum was one of our dinner ladies who went off to some other job when school was over.

I tried to explain but he wouldn't listen. A couple of paperbacks concealed under her jacket? It was nothing. And she was going to read them, wasn't she? But see his mind is made up before you begin. I mean – I do not have any influence on his world. His world is absolute.

'But if I let this one off with a caution they'll all be doing it,' he had said very reasonably, and the prosecution had gone ahead and that had been the end of it. For him.

Not, however, for me. It was months before I stopped being tried and found guilty.

But his defence was unarguable: 'I can't make one

set of rules for my daughter's friends and another for everyone else. It wouldn't be fair.'

And he was right, of course.

I just wish he understood.

8

The Evans's house is painted apricot. Its lean-to is bright with geraniums and ribbon rosettes pinned to the woodwork. As I walk round to the stable side, two collies bark a furious welcome. Alerted, one or two of the ponies push out their misleadingly grave heads, like grown-ups watching kids clowning about. The rich smell of straw and manure is attracting little clouds of evening insects. I flick ineffectually at the flies which circle and come teasingly in to land on almost the same places each time – nostrils, ears and long-suffering brown eyes. In an abstract sort of way I can understand the appeal of ponies but they are really not for me. I would swap any one of them for an emerald-green two CV with one of those rubber band engines.

'Sam! Come on in!'

Mrs Evans has that sort of leathery skin which remains tawny even in winter. Summer simply adds a burnish, an amber lustre which contrasts sharply with her short, wavy, greyish-brown hair.

'Stamp the straw off your boots first. Don't want any more of it in my kitchen than I have to. Salad and pork pie – nothing fancy. Tuck in. Help yourself.'

I am already envying Glyn this mother, so attractively functional in blue shirt and jeans and oiled leather boots. I admire the way she speaks and moves about – no dithering, no fuss, no frills and no nonsense.

Glyn looks up briefly from a Scrabble game.

''lo, Sam.'

The girl he is playing with gives me one of those bitchy, female-to-female inspections.

'That short for Samantha?'

Glyn, misinterpreting my embarrassment, says: 'Don't be daft. Samantha's a girl's name.'

'You mean you're a boy?'

'These days it's sometimes quite hard to tell the difference,' puts in Mrs Evans. I understand that she is really saying: 'Lay off Sam,' and I am grateful.

Martin, a red-haired Northerner with spectacles, picks up the conversation and sends it off in a different direction.

'Short for something, though, isn't it – Sam?'

'Samuel.' Thank God I remembered.

'What about Samson?' The dark-haired girl was still baiting me.

'Oh shut up, Louisa!'

'Rides like a female, too. Noticed it yesterday.'

'I've had enough of this old rubbish,' Mrs Evans says briskly. 'Sick and tired of it I am. I'm a lot more interested in who's going to do the washing up tonight. No, not you, Sam – you're a visitor. How's your old lady, by the way?'

'She's alright.'

'Had another of her goes at reforming the heathen of Bettws, so I'm told. A lost cause, that, I'm afraid. She could make a start with our Glyn down there, mind you.' A confused chicken, clucking and strutting with witless determination across the red and black tiles, is pounced upon and seen off: 'Shoo! Get out of here! Go on! Shoo!' She turns her attention to us and, for a moment, I think that she might be going to see me off with an equal vigour. 'Go and sort out the video then. What's it to be tonight? Not *Jaws* again I hope. . . .'

I pick up a can of Coke and settle myself down with pleasure in a room which would be my mother's nightmare. Listen – we are more country than this in London, with our Laura Ashley cottons and our herbs and dried flowers hanging from the kitchen ceiling and Mum drifting round the place in her long Sixties skirts, like some Edwardian country lady. The armchair I am curled up in now is elephantine and shapeless, part of a three piece suite covered in beige cord, threadbare and furry with dog hairs, and I like it. A couple of grubby sheepskins slump unaesthetically on the maroon and gold patterned carpet, and the tiled coffee table in front of me carries a miscellany of magazines: *Horse and Rider*, *Country Life*, *Farming Weekly* and all the locals – none of your *Homes and Gardens* stuff here.

It is odd, even exciting, to sit in front of a television set after ten days' confinement with Gwen. I would enjoy this re-make of *Startrek* a bit better, though, if I could simply relax and be my true self – this 'boy' stuff is a bit of a drag. It had been easy on the ride; I had not had to talk much, even to Glyn, and anyway I had been much too busy concentrating on staying with my pony to care. Here, though, I felt conspicuously neuter – neither easily one of the males nor yet one of the girls. Even Glyn's young brother David addressed me awkwardly, as if he did not know quite how to categorize me. I never realized until now how much of my identity is mixed up with my gender and I am not at all sure that I like the idea.

My general unease with myself is not helped by Mrs Evans.

'Whereabouts in Swansea do you come from, Sam?'

I have to respond quickly. I know just two things about Swansea – it has Dylan Thomas and a university.

'Not far from the university,' I say vaguely but that seems to satisfy her.

By eleven or so I feel that I should be getting back. At Gwen's I have fallen into the habit of going to bed ridiculously early because there is nothing else to do.

'Glyn!' Mrs Evans yells. 'Walk Sam back with the big torch. Take the short cut through the fields.'

It is really funny to be walking in the dark with a boy, without the mess of wondering if he fancies me or if he is going to make a pass.

I say: 'I really like your mum.' I mean it.

'A lot of them don't. Scares them off – a bit too blunt for them, Mam. She had to be tough, see, with us two to bring up after Dad left.'

I restrain my curiosity.

'It was nice of her to ask me over.'

'Well, it must be a bit queer for you up there in the evenings with only Gwen for company. Don't suppose for one minute she's got a telly, has she?'

'Too sinful, she told me. Hasn't even got a fridge, which is pretty awkward in this weather.'

'Well, come round here whenever you want to – no trouble for us.'

The sky is all glittery with stars again.

'You never see skies like that where I come from,' I say unguardedly.

'Oh, towns . . . all that pollution, all those street lights. . . . Look.' He switches off the torch. 'See? That's better, man. There's Orion – look. Come up here with a telescope and it's bloody marvellous. How old are you?' he asks unexpectedly.

I am cunning. 'Fifteen. Just,' I add. Nearly sixteen, as a male, might not come over too convincingly.

'So how much longer are you going to be here, then?'

'Another week or so, I suppose. . . .'

'Pretty vague about it, aren't you?'

'Thought I might hang about up here for a while. . . . I mean, it's a long holiday and we're not going away or anything. I like it up here.'

That was a mistake.

'Should come up more often then. Not difficult, is it, from Swansea? Relative up here too – though they don't bother much about Gwen, your lot, do they?'

Embarrassed, I quickly change the subject.

'You know these communes you sometimes read about?'

'Communes?'

'You know the sort of thing – people living wild, off the land, sort of colonies.'

He thinks it over.

'There's a colony of architectural students over in the valley down by Llanfair. Doing some kind of research into basic housing for the Third World. Why?'

I shrug. 'Just curious . . .'

He laughs.

71

'Orgies you're looking for, is it? All that free sex?'

I remember my role just in time and grin feebly.

'Something like that.' Really, it's all they think about.

'Louisa had a proper old go at you tonight – wonder what set her off? Bitchy cow; beats me at Scrabble most of the time too.'

'Do you,' I enquire boldly, man to man, 'fancy her?'

'Louisa? Tell me another . . . get a better screw out of a hedgehog!'

'I'm not too bad at Scrabble myself,' I say casually. 'Challenge you sometime.'

It never stays dry for long up here.

When it rains there is nothing much to do but chat up Gwen. I cannot impose myself on the Evanses so soon and, anyway, the prospect of another session of keeping up this ridiculous front is too exhausting. At least with Gwen I can relax: any mistakes I make will be forgotten in five minutes. Louisa is a different cup of tea. She already suspects, I think, that there is something funny about me, and if I am to make a complete idiot of myself, I would prefer not to do it in front of her.

So I play at entertaining Gwen, unearthing an old jigsaw puzzle and setting it up on the big wooden tray. It is not difficult to do, but I have not reckoned with her short attention span and her poor eyesight.

'Where do you think this one goes, Auntie Gwen?' I prompt, pushing her hand over in the right direction. 'There? That's right. Aren't you clever?' These days my life is so full of acting that perhaps I should go professional. . . .

After ten or so long minutes of this sort of thing I am bored and begin prodding her with questions in the fragile hope that something interesting might emerge.

'What happened to Megan's youngest?' I ask casually, as if I do not really care. The jigsaw puzzle nonsense might have softened her up sufficiently to break through her defences.

'None of your business, is it?'

'But was it,' I wheedle, guessing wildly, 'an accident?'

She sniffs.

'Some softies might call it that – I wouldn't. All over now, isn't it? A long time ago, all water under the bridge. Used to stay here a lot then, always visiting . . . nice little girl she was . . .' She turns on me, suddenly quite fierce. 'Don't you go raking up dirt from the past, young man. You're all the same, you young people of today, can't think of anything but smut. . . .'

Smut? A nice boy like me?

If it's anything to do with my mother, you bet I can't!

Whatever had she done to shock them, all those years ago, back in the Sixties? Stripped off in Chapel? Slept with the vicar? Robbed a bank? I can't help it: I just have to find out.

I mean – this house must be full of stories. . . .

On top of the wardrobe in my room, for instance, there is this cardboard box simply bulging with stuff: papers, letters, postcards, and a couple of tatty-looking scrolls tied up with string – not the legal kind, not secret wills or anything like that; more like the pictures you bring home so proudly from infants'

73

school. You must think it is awful, looking through someone else's letters and things. Under normal circumstances I would agree with you. Roz would kill me if I so much as looked at the handwriting on one of her precious postcards. In this situation, though, it feels OK.

For instance, I have to use her money, simply because I do not have any of my own and we have to eat. I mean, she does not even know it's there. I keep finding it all over the place, squirrelled away under cushions, stuffed into drawers, all mixed up with the bags of flour and the rancid butter papers and the fermenting raisins inside those old biscuit tins – once, even, in the grill pan of the stove. Grilled fivers on toast, anyone? She does not seem to be aware of money any more: the only thing she makes a fuss about now is that old brown bag.

And the bits of her life lie all around me like pieces of a puzzle. I have never known an old person before, apart from my gran and she's just my gran. Gwennie's something else.

Only the other day I came across an old postcard, tucked between the tissue-thin leaves of her big Bible so it must have, once, been important.

'Dearest Gwendolyn,' it began promisingly, but the ending: 'Hope this finds you as it leaves me, Edward,' was a bit of a damp squib. No love? No kisses?

'Who was Edward, Auntie Gwennie?' I teased.

Her expression became almost coy.

'Never you mind, boyo.' And I could swear that she blushed.

So she did have some sex in her life, after all. All those years ago, someone had fancied Gwen. I do not know why but I felt ridiculously pleased.

74

She is nodding off again. Conversation over and the rain never stops, moving in thin, horizontal sheets across the hills. My thoughts return to that cardboard box and all its mysteries. It might yield something, if only a giggle. I go up to my room and take it down.

Among the boring account books, yellowing newspapers and photographs I come across an antique version of the sort of cheap little drawing pad you give to kids to keep them occupied on long journeys. You know the sort of thing – on the cover, a simpering, rosy-cheeked 'artist' is showing off a picture of a bunch of flowers in a pot.

Here, then, might be a bit more of Gwennie's secret past. Did she draw when she was young? I remember all that skilful embroidery and think it not unlikely. Anyway, they say that artistic talent runs in families – though in that respect you can forget about me. 'Haven't inherited much of your mum's gift, have you, dear?' I remember an exquisitely sensitive teacher remarking in primary school.

Anticipating I don't know what, the usual thing: pale, crayonned flowers, ladies in elaborately pretty dresses, possibly even a watery water-colour, I flip through the pages. But this is ridiculous. By the time I am through I am gasping. I mean – these glowering landscapes, the painstaking pen-and-ink studies of rocks and boulders, that drawing of a stunted tree just clinging to the bare hillside – any one of these would have sent my art teacher over the moon. The stuff is childish; I mean, it is amateur and not impressively finished like Mum's things: it's just impressive. There is even a sketchy self-portrait – the younger Gwen? She looks about forty but the face is clearly recognizable.

75

Right now, this find completely eclipses the possible petty crimes of my dear mother as a girl. Here is this totally unexpected piece of Gwen and I want to know more. Maybe she had wanted to be an artist and her brother wouldn't let her: brother John sounds like a bit of a creep to me and I wouldn't put it past him. I want to make it right. I know it sounds silly but I want her to feel appreciated.

I run downstairs and wave the book at her just as Miss Matthias opens the door.

My excited, 'Look what I've found!' dies before the Matthias's, 'Hello, Gwen – how are we today? Let me have a good look at you. Sam, a nice pot of tea, there's a good boy.'

Chastened by our last conversation I slink away like a well-trained cur. When I come back with tea and biscuits on a tray, she is into her sales pitch once again. This time I stay out of it.

'Remember Olwen? Olwen Price the Chapel? Used to do the flowers and clean up . . . proper artist with her flower arrangements. . . .'

'A stuck-up article, that Olwen,' Gwen comments drily.

'Well, she's done very well for herself now.' Miss Matthias is relentless. 'Gone into the Eventide . . . says it was the best move she ever made.'

'Best place for her, too, at her age.' Gwen's unexpected bitchiness has me almost laughing out loud. There is more to my aunt than you would ever suspect.

I cannot wait to show her my discovery. Almost before Miss Matthias is out of the door I push it into her lap.

'Look.'

'What's this old rubbish you've got hold of, then?' Just what she would say, of course.

I open it for her carefully, treating it with the respect I feel it deserves, turning the pages slowly so that she can study them. She says nothing. Maybe she is embarrassed. I encourage her a bit.

'Remember doing these?' She smiles wetly and shakes her head at me. 'I think they're fantastic,' I add; I do not want her to think that I am laughing at her.

'Love you. . . .' She drops the book on the floor. 'I couldn't draw water from a well. . . . Hers, these are . . . should have got rid of all that old rubbish years ago.'

'Whose?'

'My little niece's. Never stops drawing when she comes up here . . . keeps her out of mischief.'

I feel cheated.

'Which niece is that?' I ask faintly, anticipating the reply.

'Oh you know . . . that little girl of Megan's . . . Our Winnie . . .'

I wish to hell that Our Winnie could stay out of my life.

I travel two hundred miles, hitch, find myself a brilliant hide-away, fool half the population into thinking that I am a boy, only to meet up with my mother's ghost? Look – what has she to do with me, this long-ago girl? Disturbed, probably. She would have to be to make drawings like that. I mean – they bother me, those bloody drawings. I mean – a nice little scandal would have been something else: I could have coped with that.

Look – my mother's inner life is not my business. I have enough problems of my own.

9

Last night I had a nightmare.

I dreamed that I was posing for my mother, sprawled over an armchair in jeans and a tee shirt. I was flipping through a magazine and watching the lines grow; watching someone drawing always has this hypnotic effect on me and I can never look away for very long.

The pencilled eyes seemed to stare out at me, upside-down. Suddenly they were my own eyes. I tried to blink but she had drawn them open.

And she was smiling at me.

'Dreadful haircut,' she was saying, 'but we can easily sort that out for you,' and pencilled ringlets began to curl out of my own skull and grow around my neck.

'No,' I tried to say. 'Stop it,' but she was drawing my lips and they were closed.

Then she was holding me away from her, critical, frowning. She sighed.

'Not one of my best. . . .'

When she reached for the rubber I began to scream.

I sleep late and wake up past noon still thick with sleep and moist between the legs. I recognize that

78

familiar ache in the pit of my stomach: my period has come. I clean myself up as best I can – with a spongeful of icy water at the kitchen sink – and make myself some hot coffee. My stomach hurts. Irritably I wonder how many drawers and little boxes I will have to go through before I find some aspirin. Quicker to walk down to the village.

Gwen comes nosing in, shuffling in slippers, the buttons on her pinafore dress all mismatched, and scrapes a kitchen chair across my headache. I set a cup of milky coffee in front of her.

'There's funny to see a boy so handy in the kitchen.'

I am not in the mood, and if I have heard this pearl of wisdom once, I have heard it a hundred times.

'Silly old cow,' I snap. 'Why don't you say something different for once?'

Here eyes go all swimmy.

'Don't you speak to me like that,' she protests weakly, 'or I'll have to tell tales to your mam.' The hand with the cup is shaking and slopping the coffee all over the plastic cloth.

'That,' I reply icily, 'might be a little difficult, Auntie Gwen. If not bloody impossible.'

My unpleasantness brings me a sort of relief but I do not like myself. I am not a nice person. I do the same thing with Mum sometimes, catching her off guard and watching her dissolve into slush.

To a plaintive cry of 'Ooh the language!', I get the hell out of there.

By the time I arrive at the shop I am altogether disgusted with myself; I am not fit for human company. With my purchased loot, a copy of *The Face*, two months old, a newspaper, a can of Coke to wash down the aspirins, a currant bun and a bagful of windfalls, I head for open pasture, aiming to pass out in the heather for the afternoon.

I get as far as the deserted churchyard around Ebenezer Chapel and drop like a stone into the long grass. After a while I wriggle up against the grey plinth of the angel they call Gwennie's, eat my bun and knock back the aspirins. Behind me, above my head, flies this angel, hair streaming, wings frozen in an upward beat, robe, even in full flight, modestly draped over outstretched legs. I wish he would help me, too; tell me what to do next; tell me what to do with my life. I mean – any ambition I might finally excavate will probably die in the dole queue. . . .

Blown dandelions stand upright in the grass like snuffed-out candles and beyond the confines of grim little Ebenezer and its neglected garden the rust and lavender hills hump like beasts. Drowsy, I curl up among the green-smelling dock leaves and the sun spins rings of gold around my eyes and this funny little rhyme comes into my head. . . . 'I am afraid of the power of my mother and the weakness of my father . . . I am afraid of the power of my father and the weakness of my mother'. . . . I must have come across something like it in a book. Gibberish, really.

When I wake up, my stomach-ache has all gone. Gratefully I roll over and begin to leaf dumbly through the magazine, and eventually I find enough strength to stumble, a fat cow among the gravestones, musing over epitaphs, back towards the road. Kids have defaced some of the statues. Leaving, I turn to admire the full countenance of Gwennie's angel and find that he is wearing spectacles, crudely scribbled in bright blue felt-tip. He looks like a bank

80

clerk in drag. I am shocked. I mean – nobody's angel should be grounded like that. Especially hers. Some day soon I will have to come back and do a clean-up job on him.

Feeling more human now, I decide to go over to the Evanses in search of a bit of normality. There is just so much I can take of old women and angels. A twinge of guilt comes close to sending me right back to the cottage but I suppress it. I can apologize later – if she remembers the incident at all. She'll be alright. I mean, she managed before I came and she will manage after I have left, so why fuss?

Mrs Evans is mucking out the stables when the dogs announce my presence; there is no one else around. She looks up, her grey-brown hair damp with sweat.

'Oh hullo, Sam. Missed them, I'm afraid – off all afternoon on a long ride. Be back in an hour or so, I should think.'

I am about to leave but she stops me.

'Wait, why don't you? Lemonade in the fridge – go over and help yourself. Join you in a minute. I'm sweating like a pig in this old heat.'

I go to the kitchen and tentatively remove an orange plastic jug from the fridge. I am shy in other people's houses, always afraid of doing something wrong or breaking something. It would be sensible for me to take down a couple of tumblers from the scratched green dresser but the shelves are so crowded that I daren't take the risk.

Mrs Evans sighs.

'Put out a couple of glasses, Sam, do,' she orders impatiently, splashing water over her hands and face. 'Unless you want to drink it straight from the jug. . . .'

Soft sunlight plays over a grey honeycomb of eggboxes stacked up against the window, and dapples a clump of drooping marigolds in a jampot still labelled *Plum and Apple*. On the wall, horse brasses, glinting copper, hang between galvanized iron tubs, and, over a battered wickerwork chair, a ginger and white cat droops like an Oxfam fur coat. I begin to imagine what my mother and her friends might do to this nice room, stripping the dresser back to its original pine, filling the place with dried flowers and making still-lifes out of the apples and the ripening green and red tomatoes. I can just see the shelves groaning with earthenware, and Habitat blinds at the window. Trouble is – I quite like those kinds of things myself. . . .

'Penny for them?'

'Oh . . . nothing really. . . . You've got lots of photos of horses, haven't you?' I comment brightly, indicating the snapshots pinned to the side of the dresser.

'Horses in the kitchen, people in the lounge. Everything in its proper place, see. Glyn and David and their dad all framed on top of the piano. Tell you, it's more peaceful out here. . . .'

Shocked by her bitterness I can find nothing of any value to say, especially as a boy, but the moment passes, dissolving like a summer cloud.

'They're off swimming tomorrow, I believe.' She is brisk and practical again. 'Twenty-mile ride up to some old freezing puddle – not my cup of tea at all, I can tell you, but you might enjoy it.'

I shudder at the thought. At this moment what I need is a hot water bottle. 'No thanks!' I say with feeling.

82

She gives me this penetrating look which makes me wriggle.

'Too risky is it, swimming?'

I protest at this.

'Acutally I'm quite a good swimmer.'

'It wasn't that kind of risk I was thinking of – not what I had in mind at all. Just reminded of what Louisa said the other night. . . .'

I am horrified.

'All that nonsense about me being a girl?' My indignation sounds fakey even to me.

'If all that nonsense just happened to be true, though, the last thing in the world you'd want to do would be to go swimming. . . . Oh, don't look so upset, Sam: I was only teasing, only trying you out. But all the same, there's something fishy about you – no offence meant, but something not quite right. . . . Doesn't stop me liking you, mind, but I prefer people to be straight with me right from the start, see – Here they come. Boots outside if you please!' she shouts, all the intimate stuff over. 'Lemonade in here if you want it. Chop up some more lemons, Sam, there's a good boy.'

Her slight emphasis on the word 'boy' makes me feel that even if her suspicions turn out to be true she will not betray me.

Scrabble-playing is possibly my only talent. I deliberately take on Louisa. This girl needs deflating.

'Coming swimming tomorrow, Sam?' she teases. 'Show off your boobs to everyone?'

'Why not?' I reply calmly and that shuts her up for a while.

'I'll play the winner,' announces Glyn. He has been keeping an eye on the game and Louisa's defeat has obviously pleased him.

'Fill up one of those boxes with eggs for the old lady before you go, Sam – do her the world of good. Laid only yesterday – none of your old battery rubbish round here.'

'Thanks, Mrs Evans.'

'Don't you "Mrs Evans" me. I've got a name, you know; call me Jinnie like everyone else does.'

'Thanks then, Jinnie.'

The others drift away, some inevitably back to the stables to drool afresh over the ponies. Occasionally I hear Jinnie's voice, clear and tough as plate glass: 'Leave her, now – leave her. She's had enough spoiling for one day.'

Scrabble does not foster much of what you might describe as meaningful conversation; however, my thoughts were only partly on the game. Frankly, I was worried.

'Been talking to your mum. . . .'

'Oh yes,' he says abstractedly, his eyes on the possibility of a treble score.

'Seems to think I'm a bit of an oddball,' I say carefully, watching his face.

'Don't take any notice . . . bit paranoid, our mam.'

'Glyn. . . .'

'M-m-m-m?'

'Do *you* think I'm an oddball?'

'Everyone's a bloody oddball once you get to know them.'

I spell out VIRGIN, pushing up my score by sixty. He groans.

'That what you are, then?'

'What?'

He grins. 'Not had it yet, then?'

I pick up his implication.

'Honk If You Had It Last Night!' I neatly deflect the question by quoting a car sticker. It works. We both laugh. 'Don't make any assumptions, though.'

I am held up by four A's and no inspiration.

'Glyn. . . .'

'Can't you see I'm thinking?'

'But I want to ask you something.' I have to keep pushing.

He bangs his knuckles against his forehead.

'You're no better than Louisa. Just the same. . . .'

'In which way?' I ask quickly.

'Distracting me all the bloody time. That's her technique, too. That's why she always beats me. It's Glyn this and Glyn that. . . . Sabotage, that's what I call it.'

I lose the game. I am the one who is distracted.

The greying fields are smudged with bronze as I walk back, clutching my box of eggs, and the hills are all velvet-dark against a gaudy sky.

The cottage is silent but when I go upstairs I find her fast asleep against a mess of pillows, mouth open and gently snoring.

'Auntie Gwen?' I say. I hate the way old people look dead when they're just asleep. My gran looks like that sometimes.

She gulps, teeth clacking, and opens one eye.

'Sam? Oh there's glad I am to see you.' She heaves herself round in the bed. 'Such a rude boy came in here this morning . . . oooh the language. . . . I soon sent him packing, though.'

10

I have written to Ranjit. It is about time I dropped her a line; she deserves something, and, anyway, I need to be honest with someone.

Dear Ranjit (*I wrote*),
Bet you'll be surprised to get this!
   Thanks a lot for your help. You were great! I did go down to Pauline's that night but she's probably told you that by now. Afterwards I went off on my own, hitching cross-country. It's a bit scary and you've got to be careful but it does get you places for free.
   Right now I'm doing odd jobs and living rough. I'm OK.
   Passed through this village today – hence the postmark. [*Well, I am only too familiar with Ranjit's destructive honesty and I have to think of everything.*] I will, of course, have moved on by the time you get this.
   I suppose I'm being a sort of tramp. [*I wish this bit were true!*] Up to now I've been a kind of general help to this rich old lady [*that's a joke!*] who feeds me and all that.
   Freedom is great and I don't regret doing what I

did in spite of what you said. You should try it yourself sometime before your parents marry you off!!

See you sometime.
Love, Cealie

Jinnie Evans is too smart for me. I am going to have to come clean with her: I wonder how she is going to take it? How is she going to deal with a Sam who re-defines himself as a Cealie? And what about Glyn? People are a bit like chess pieces; change a knight into a rook and you have a totally different game. I will simply have a different mask, but I'm the same person inside. At least, I think that I am but I'm not really sure; when I'm being Sam I feel different.

Maybe people look at each other through masks all the time, and never really see each other at all; I have this frightening image of a Mother mask, a Dad mask and even a Roz mask. It sounds ridiculous but, right now, I cannot cope with the possibility of things familiar, I mean – people I have known all my life, suddenly growing new faces.

I should never have grubbed around in that cardboard box. None of my business, was it? Now I can't leave it alone. I have lifted it down once again, carefully, so as not to scatter its gerbils' nest of rubbish. Here is an exercise book, its blue covers dry and curled, full of the sort of goo that Roz would write: names with little hearts or daggers scribbled around them, beauty hints cut out from magazines, a couple of sentimental poems and the odd recipe. The drawing book I fussed over the other day has fallen to the ground. I flip through it again. It is really not so hot. Some of Roz's stuff – when I'm allowed to see it – is far better.

The last few pages are covered in scribbled notes. I hadn't bothered with them the first time round. Now I am curious. At first glance they are just technical jottings, notes for a painting, disjointed, messy, the kind of thing that makes sense only to the writer: 'raw sienna lightened with white . . . sky and lake both the same tone . . . Payne's Grey . . . try Chrome Yellow . . . purply ultramarine in the shadows.'

Then, disconcertingly, it turned into something else, something crazy, a sort of mad poetry.

'Bones of the earth, mangled and twisted . . . The rock bones all bleached where they surface . . . In my mouth and nostrils the breath of the hills – yellow scent and brown spice . . . Those tufts of straw that grow diagonally are just like the tuft between my legs which I look at in her long mirror . . . There's wicked, she'd say. There's bad you are. Oh I am a dirty girl, writing it down. What if she found it?

'She says, "Why don't you paint flowers instead of all that old rubbish?" Auntie Gwennie is all dried up . . . I'm sorry for her and I hate her old brother-husband, sucking on his pipe while she dances attendance on him . . . and I hate their rotten little chapel. Jesus loves them? He can have them. Gareth loves me, see, and I love Gareth and nobody knows. . . . Gareth can touch me anywhere he likes I wish he would but if he did I would say No No No like the rest of them, don't make yourself cheap now Freda . . . easy come easy go. Why won't she stop calling me Winnie? She prefers Nancy anyway. . . .'

The demons are dancing inside my head. Who is she? Who is this strange, passionate girl who has

88

broken, like a thief, into my life? My mother?

It isn't Mum; it couldn't be. I mean, Mum has this fey personality. I remember once, as a little girl, finding one of her long patchwork skirts wreathed on the bathroom floor and still warm, as if the body inside it had simply evaporated and left it behind like a discarded cocoon, and I thought that she had flown away just like a butterfly, disappeared for ever, and I cried and cried.

I still have this fantasy about her dying: one day she will flutter away and I will watch her growing smaller and smaller until she becomes like a mote that dances before my eyes.

Bits of her are floating inside my head right now. 'Your mum's a fairy lady,' some kid at infants' school once said to me, wistfully, after one of her story-reading sessions in the little store room behind the shop. ('Catch them young', Dad was always saying.) There she would sit, centre of attention – she was always a good reader – swathed in her skirts like Mother Goose, all necklaces and rings and eccentric spectacles slipping down her slender nose, something from a Christmas pantomime. More frequently now it's: 'Your mum's a nutcase.' These days she even wears two pairs of spectacles for drawing – bi-focals, she feels, are a bit too elderly – and there she sits, her multiple eyes all out of focus, like a cross between a lacewing and a leprechaun.

But you see I love her. I mean – it's a reflex: I don't have any choice. If I'd had a choice in the matter I would not have picked her in the first place. I just want a mum like everyone else's. . . .

Now I am not so sure about what might lie behind even a mum like everyone else's. . . .

I shake myself free of all this nonsense and pile the stuff back inside the box. There is something I have to do.

I pick my time carefully, knowing that the rest of them will have left on the swimming expedition.

She was in the yard, scrubbing away at the windscreen of the Land Rover.

'Bloody old flies,' she grumbles, as if I had been there all the time. 'Windscreen's like a battlefield! Bit late for the ride, aren't you? They left hours ago.'

'I actually came to see you,' I say awkwardly.

'There's bad timing for you then. I'm just off to Llanrwst to pick up a few things. Come with me if you've got nothing better to do. Can't promise any excitement but there's a good cake shop if you're interested . . . home-made stuff, bread pudding and cream, that sort of thing. Bad for your figure but then you men don't worry about that sort of thing and I don't have a figure to spoil.'

Is there a certain irony in the way she says, 'you men'?

'That'd be nice.'

'Hop in then.' The two dogs, when she switches on the engine, begin circling around us, barking wildly. 'Know they're being left behind and they're hopping mad! Love driving, those two . . . one of these days they're going to work out how to do it for themselves. You drive?'

Driving lessons are always being proposed by me and postponed by them. The present declaration stands at 'on your eighteenth birthday'. That feels like never.

'Not yet, but I want to.'

90

'Like to take this beast out as far as the lane for me?'

Aghast, I protest: 'But I've never—' This is not entirely true; when we rented a cottage last year, my dad let me drive the Cortina at a snail's pace a little way down the private road, but a Land Rover is something else. . . .

We swap seats. This is crazy. I move dumbly.

'Now don't you worry too much about the steering; she's built like a battleship and she's not going to wander.' Jinnie straps me in and stuffs a couple of old cushions down behind my back. She is one of those people who simply take you over. 'Left foot on the clutch and into gear – that's my boy . . .' We begin to move forward, very slowly. For the moment all my other worries are forgotten: they are all rolled up inside this one. 'Don't bother about the dogs,' she says when I hesitate. 'Got more sense than most people.'

This is me, up here like a god, controlling this big machine. I am seriously considering the possibility of becoming a long-distance lorry driver when she yells, 'Brakes! Neutral. Handbrake. Right, Sam, I'll take over now. You did well, boyo.'

The warm air fans my cheeks and the growing stubble on my head as we start climbing. The road is quite empty. Little clouds brush the swelling land like dark wings. Cropping ponies, disturbed by our racket, shy away into the bracken. The steep meadows down below the Forestry Plantation are pebbled with sheep.

'In for a bit of rain later,' Jinnie remarks after a long silence.

By now I am right back with my problem. Is it

really necessary to tell her? And how could I say it? 'I'm actually a girl, you see,' sounds too inane.

'Jinnie. . . .'

'M-m-m-m?'

'You know what you were saying the other day? About there being something not quite right about me? Well, I think I ought to tell you . . .' and here I go all to pieces, '. . . only it's sort of secret you see and a bit embarrassing and Miss Matthias thinks I'm a boy.'

'A bit simple in some respects, our Doris,' says Jinnie shortly. 'Easily taken in, so don't flatter yourself. Why the "boy" act then?'

This is even more difficult. I have to feel quite sure that I can trust her.

'Will you promise not to tell anyone?' It sounds melodramatic and silly. 'Not even Glyn?'

'That would depend. . . .' There is a small silence while she considers my request. I like Jinnie. She doesn't piss around and she takes me seriously. Maybe, though, it is Sam she respects. I don't think she has much time for girls.

'You don't seem to be doing any actual harm up here,' she says at last, and I can see her thinking it all out. 'Don't know what you're living on though . . . family well-off, I take it. Come to think of it, as far as the old lady's concerned you've done quite a bit of good . . . proud of her young man, so Doris Matthias tells me. Better not say anything to Gwennie, poor soul – she's confused enough as it is with her visions of angels. . . . Think your heart's in the right place, though not everyone would. You're OK by me, Sam. Can't call you that now, can I? What's your real name?'

'Cealie.' I could call myself anything but I'm tired of lies.

'Alright then . . . Cealie. What's it all about?'

We rattle thunderously across a cattle ford.

I am about to give her the 'my mother threw me out' line but I check myself. Even I did not really believe that story any more.

'I've left home.' It sounds so much more dignified and gives me some choice in the matter. 'Sort of run away, if you can call it that at my age.'

'How old are you, then?'

'Sixteen.' Well, it's almost true.

'Parent problems?'

'I suppose you could call it that.'

'Don't get on, is it? Scrapping all the time and you've had enough?'

I am shocked.

'Oh no – nothing like that.' I mean, I can't imagine them fighting. I have rarely heard them arguing. There is very little violence in my family apart from my own.

'I'm glad for you. Rotten for kids when it gets like that. Some people battle on but there's no point in it really; better to make a clean break, for everyone's sake.'

'Was it like that—?'

'With Glyn's father? Yes.' I wish I had not mentioned it but she does not seem to mind. 'Oh, yes . . . you're talking to an old hand at that game, my girl (there's funny calling you that). My fault too, mind – nobody's blameless in these situations and don't you forget it. Knew what I was letting myself in for from the start: I was no innocent, I can tell you. . . . Never really saw eye to eye, me and Gareth,

93

except in bed and sometimes not even there. Not a bad man, mind you – just what you might call a womanizer. Always looking for something just out of sight, over the rainbow . . . hasn't found it yet. I'm the faithful old sheepdog type, see – couldn't stand it. That's enough about my troubles; now what about you?'

We pull up in a lane at the back of the Farmer's Arms – no parking problems here.

'I just – wanted to get away,' I say lamely, wishing I had some dreadful tale to tell. 'I got my hair cut.' It sounds sillier and sillier but I flounder on. 'It used to be long and very curly and I couldn't stand it. My mother objected in a big way . . . there was a row and I walked out.'

'I see. . . . Look, business now; we'll talk about it properly later over a couple of jam tarts.'

I follow her into the main street and in and out of various shops, feeling about as helpful as a three-year-old, hanging back while she orders vitamins and various feeds for the horses and trying to look intelligent during her long, technical conversation with the warehouseman. I am convinced that she has totally forgotten my existence when she turns and dismisses me with , 'Get a move on, Sam. Meet you at the Copper Kettle at four.'

It is a big deal, Llanrwst: the wicked Metropolis. Hard to know what to look at first. I gawp at a display of refined and over-priced summer dresses protected against the vulgarity of sunlight by a sheet of yellowing polythene. The narrow street is as intimate as a room. I pick up funny, dissected snatches of conversation: 'Vi-let? Where's Vi-let then?' . . . 'There'll be blood on the moon if I don't get one.' . . .

'Ych-y-fi don't do that.' . . . The Welsh voices rise and fall like the cooing of doves. I contemplate a collection of tweed caps and Artic socks; I thrill to a display of best galvanized buckets, vermin-destroying powders and a lurid poster about worming sheep.

Finally I pick up a romantic novel at the stationer's, lean against the window-ledge of the Copper Kettle and wallow in passion. At twenty-past four she still hasn't arrived. I am worried. Have I said too much, opened my big mouth too wide? Is she talking; ringing the police, perhaps?

At last she comes striding up the street, breathless, late and unapologetic.

'What you doing down here? Expected to find you upstairs stuffing your face with cream buns.'

I follow her like a puppy.

At the top of the steep wooden stairs is an afternoon sort of room where the sun slips in around the scarlet and salmon-pink geraniums and makes glistening pools over the pock-marked linoleum. At the small event of our arrival conversation dips perceptibly and female eyes give us the quick once-over. A middle-aged woman, bulging in a strawberry trousersuit, is working her way solemnly through a large ice-cream.

'Tea for two, is it?' A plump, smiling woman in a flowered overall finds us a table. 'Hullo, Mrs Evans, turned out nice again today.'

Jinnie wastes no time on small talk.

'So why Gwen?' she launches on me.

I gulp.

'Convenience, I suppose,' I say at last. It sounds awful when I put it like that.

'And not all that far to come . . . hitch?'

I nod.

'Well it can't go on for much longer, you know. Apart from the state she's in, people are going to talk. . . . Talking already, some of them.'

'Saying what?'

She gives an exasperated sigh. 'Saying? What do you expect them to say – use your loaf. "There's a funny old lot they must be then, sending that kid off to stay with poor old Gwennie Davies who's half way out of her tree. Lot of parasites, that's what they are . . . never come near her themselves. . ."'

'My family?' I ask dumbly, not even trying to be defensive.

'Who else, boyo?'

Tea arrives in silver pots and fluted white crockery. The silver cakestand bears marbled pudding, treacle tarts, chocolate hedgehogs and cauliflower-shaped cream buns dredged in icing sugar. I do not feel hungry.

'Told your mam where you are?'

'No.'

'She must be out of her mind with worry then.'

'I've rung her,' I say crossly. 'Told her I'm OK. Several times, in fact.'

'You were my girl, that wouldn't be enough. I'd want an address for one thing.'

They are all the same, I think wearily. I change the subject.

'Have you told Glyn?'

'Told Glyn what?'

'That you thought I was a girl.'

'Why should I? And I won't, neither. Let him find out for himself; he's got eyes in his head, same as me.'

'You going to turn me in?'

'Don't be so daft. . . . But you'll have to get yourself sorted out. Mam works?' she asks on the way out.

'She's an artist.'

'Teaches, does she?'

'No. She does illustrations and things; birthday cards . . .'

'Nice work if you can get it and if you've got the gift. Dad's the breadwinner then?'

'He runs a bookshop.'

'Oh yes, very nice, whereabouts?'

I suddenly remember that I come from Swansea.

'Near the university.' I say quickly and that seems to satisfy her. It fits in nicely with my previous story. Anyway, I have had enough of honesty for one afternoon.

'It must be quite tough,' I break an uncomfortable silence, 'running things on your own.'

'I get by. Always take it out on the boys when things get too bad. . . .' We are leaving the fine weather behind us in the valley. Up here the clouds have been building up and the first pinpricks of rain are stabbing the windscreen. 'Glyn's my problem baby – too much of his dad's blood in him. Good brain, could do well for himself, but he wants to drop out, form some kind of acting group . . . busking, see, in the streets. Load of silly old nonsense if you ask me. There, you don't want to hear about my problems; you've got enough of your own.'

People, I think again, are never what they seem.

'Want to stop over? They'll be back in a couple of hours.'

'I ought to check on Auntie Gwennie,' I reply a bit smugly. I need to think.

97

She runs me back to the cottage. The rain has become quite heavy and the sky is steaming off the backs of the hills.

'You'd better stay a Sam when you come to us. Don't want to complicate things any more. That Madam Louisa goes home tomorrow and the others couldn't care less.' With unexpected warmth she puts out her hand and ruffles what is left of my hair. 'You're alright, boyo,' she says.

The house feels disconcertingly empty.

Thinking that she might be asleep I run upstairs, but the magpie's nest she usually occupies is flat. Oh God, another trip! Remembering the defaced angel in the churchyard, I grab an anorak and run out into the garden to check before going for help. This time I know I can count on Jinnie.

But out there is Gwennie, shining wet, knee-deep in a jungle of rhubarb leaves, and gazing up at the apple tree like a kid with a crush.

'Auntie Gwennie, you're soaked!'

She turns and offers me a bleary smile.

'I have found favour in the eyes of the Lord.'

I take off my coat and put it round her shoulders.

'Go inside; it's bucketing down – you'll catch cold,' I say, but she won't budge.

'Look, Sam. He's up there in all his glory.'

All I can see are dripping leaves and hard little apples, and all I get for my pains is an eyeful of rain. I try shifting her but she is rooted to the spot and I am too nervous to attempt picking her up and carrying her.

She introduces me.

'This is Sam, my young man,' she announces, 'That's my angel,' she whispers proudly.

98

'He's beautiful!' Well, what else can I say?

'We are all labourers in God's vineyard, Sam, you see.' Well, I did not disagree. 'Woe, woe to the ungodly, saith the Lord of Hosts. I am called to preach the gospel unto the heathen, Sam.'

'Not in the rain.'

'Go down to the ungodly . . .'

I have a sudden inspiration.

'Why don't you start with me?'

'Start what?'

'Auntie Gwennie,' I declare solemnly. 'I am a sinner.'

She frowns.

'That old busybody'll be along any minute.'

'Which old busybody?'

'That Matthias woman – never could stand her . . .'

'Then why don't you hide?'

'Hide?'

'Where she won't find you. Look – in here.'

She is inside the house, wet, tired and confused.

I try to remove her cardigan, wet as a dishrag, but she snaps at me: 'Leave me alone, boyo; stop your old fussing; like an old woman you are. . . . I can look after myself; I'm not helpless.'

I give up. I *am* helpless. I put on the kettle and make us both some tea. She is gloating now, eyes shining.

'You saw him, Sam.' It is a statement, not a question. I nod.

'Beautiful he is, my angel . . . all white and wonderful . . . wings like an eagle's. Old Matthias can't see him at all – thinks I'm daft in the head.'

I bring out a towel and dry off her hair. This time

she does not protest. We are conspirators, Gwennie and I.

'Tricked her,' she chuckles. 'Tricked her, you and I. . . .'

I talk her out of some of her wet things – she is quite docile now – and somehow get her upstairs and into bed. I mean, old people can get chills and things and I don't want to be responsible.

I mean – what if she died?

11

I sat and watched the rain silently weeping over the windows. At last the clouds brightened, and an evening sun, a watery orange, came rolling out of the grey. Like a little kid I went out into the garden in search of a rainbow.

I was actually feeling rather pleased with myself. I had driven a Land Rover, talked frankly to Jinnie and stage-managed Gwennie with impressive brilliance – not bad for one day.

When I put myself to bed I lay awake for ages having funny thoughts. So Glyn wanted to be an actor. I would never have guessed – I thought actors were more extrovert – but good luck to him. He was going to need it: not many actors had jobs. Oh God, now I was thinking like her. Who the hell was she to say? Who the hell was I?

That bit about God creating people in his own image – weren't they thinking about parents when they wrote that?

At least Jinnie was honest about it. Mum said things like: 'I don't care what you do as long as you're happy,' and then made all those conditions:

'So long as your pretty curls aren't trimmed.'

'So long as you get your A levels and go to university.'

A rhythmic braying puts to flight my dream-theatre of nonsense – Gwen flying over Bettws in her grubby pink dressing gown; Jinnie in one of Mum's Victorian costumes trying to muck out the stables, and this fair-haired boy – could it have been Glyn? – trying to make a pass at me.

It is late and the day is already stale. The sun suffocates behind a pillow of cloud and the flat white light silvers the edges of the cracks in the grimy window-pane and face-powders dust all over the wardrobe mirror.

The noise goes on and on. I track it to Gwen's room and find her asleep on her back, mouth agape and nose streaming, bubbling and snorting like a drowning donkey. I mop up some of the mess with tissues, turn her over and tuck her down. Evidently she has a cold. Is it surprising?

I pull on my jeans and one of those baggy sweatshirts which has helped to back up my act. On impulse, I open the top drawer and there it is, my bag of hair. Funny, it has become increasingly like a relic – the hair of some long-forgotten princess whose life ran tick-tock according to rules no one now remembers. Nothing to do with Sam.

Yesterday's revelations were a bit much for me. I have had enough. Today I want to be private – no Jinnie, no Glyn and certainly no Gwennie. I make some cheese and tomato sandwiches, collect a miscellany of things with which to pass the time, take a last look at my snuffling auntie, and make for the hills.

The grounds looks deceptively solid but the grass

is still sequinned with rain and I find myself playing hop-scotch between island clumps spiked with reeds – one false move and I am ankle-deep in emerald slime. Grateful now for Uncle John's archaeological boots, I cautiously trip it down to the stream.

I sit on a dry stone to eat my lunch. Tomato seeds, amoeba-like in their jelly, plop on to the bare rock. I bring out my book. Scrubby sheep seem to suckle the sodden hillside as I follow the erotic escapades of the blue-eyed heroine. I try to involve myself with the plot. Should Jill submit to the advances of the unscrupulous but possibly useful film director in order to get that longed-for break? I mean – would I? Would I pay for something I really wanted by sleeping with someone? I suppose you could say, if you wanted to be bitchy, that I did just that at the party: I used him to satisfy my curiosity. It's funny – from the way they talk there are very few virgins left in my class but if you sleep around they still call you a slag. Curiosity does seem to be a very trivial reason for losing one's virginity but if you are not, actually, in love with anyone, how else do you learn about sex?

I mean, really learn. Not the stuff they give you in books. 'An orgasm', I remember reading somewhere, 'is an exciting tickly feeling.' Like hell it is. And passion?

Those drawings, those scribbled notes, have something to do with that. Was she really Mum, that girl? Was she still alive, somewhere, under all the other things? Could I find her? And how would I go about it? Crudely? Teasing? 'Mum, who was Gareth?'

Gareth. . . . A bit of yesterday's conversation with Jinnie comes into my head. 'Never really saw eye to eye, me and Gareth, except in bed. Not a bad man, mind you . . . just a womanizer.' What if . . .? Oh my God it is just too ridiculous but what if . . .? Jinnie and Mum are about the same age and they both have connections with the same bit of south Wales. It is not out of the question. . . .

The more I think about it the more fascinating the possibility becomes. Freda and Gareth. Cealie and Glyn? There is a terrible, magical logic to it, like a circle locked against time, like a serpent swallowing its own tail. . . .

The metallic blare of music makes me drop my book. High on my own thoughts, I had blanked out even the sound of the motorbike engines, but the music cannot be ignored. Neither can the two bikers on the bridge, all glittery and menacing under the candlewax sky.

They must have seen me, but as yet they are showing no signs of it. Why should they bother, anyway? To them I hope I am just a scruffy kid, splashing and stumbling upstream with his plastic bagful of junk.

I hope that is how they see me.

I can hear the snap of beer-cans opening and, turning cautiously, faking indifference, I see one of them standing midstream. The sing-song lilt of their Welsh voices seems curiously out of character with their macho image until snatches of the old, familiar crudities come drifting downwind. As a boy I am probably safe. As a girl I would almost certainly be bait, a stimulus to coarse suggestions and showing off, at the very least. It isn't fair. I work my way slowly upstream, not running, as flight might make them suspicious, or the gyrations of my bottom suggest to them that their farm boy might turn out to be a good lay.

They are splashing and fooling about in the water. Listen, I am not scared. I mean, they are probably quite harmless really but I am alone. One of them is peeing, leaning over backwards so that the stream rises in a shining arc, and laughing: they are just stupid kids. Like a Peeping Tom I ogle his penis – a pink sausage against the black and silver vee of his legs, nothing to write home about. I wouldn't want one of those except, of course, in the right place, and sometimes I doubt whether I really want one there.

I scramble gratefully down a dip in the land and they drop out of sight, but there is still no real safety: they are still there, not so very far away; their music still thrashes the air and their voices are clearly audible. I wonder how it feels to be truly male, to walk free without this niggling fear of sexual harassment – this I envy them. . . .

My imagination suddenly shoots into top gear. I am convinced that the music is louder, closer, that the splashes and shouts signify that they are wading rapidly upstream through the shallow water, that they will be on me, literally, at any moment. I had vaguely planned an escape route; concealed by the swell of the hill I would turn back and gradually retrace my path towards the top and over it to the cottage. Now the memory of my previous clumsy progress, heavy-booted across the drenched and boggy ground, fills me with foreboding. Now all my mother's fantasies about rape come horribly alive in me and I see them, striding easily over the land in their polished leather boots; I hear their laughter, smell their stale, beery breath as they force me down in the heather, knife-blade glinting menace. . . .

So lost am I in this nightmare that I cry out when the horse comes galloping up out of nowhere.

'Hi, Sam – it's only me!'

It is Glyn, riding across the hills like a rescuing knight. I feel such a fool.

'Off hiking again, are you?' The question is meaningless; it is just something to say. He is already moving off.

Like an idiot I offer up my plastic bag.

'Want a sandwich?' I offer desperately. I need him. He looks mildly surprised.

'OK.' He reins in his horse and jumps down. 'What's in them, then – smoked salmon and caviar?'

'You'd be lucky . . . just cheese and tomato.'

He bites thoughtfully into my mess of dry cheese and dangling tomato slices.

'What's the big panic then?'

'Panic?'

'You were waving that bag of yours under my nose like an offering to a bloody god, man.'

I have no choice now. I have to come clean.

'I was scared . . .'

'Of what? Those yobbos down there, is it?' His assumption is underlined by the loud revving of engines. 'Bark worse than their bite. Live inside their own little world, that lot – never bother us. They're off now – see? No loss, mind. No objections to Heavy Metal in the right place but not up here. . . . Nervous little bloke then, aren't you?'

There is such a tongue-in-cheek feeling about that last comment I am convinced Jinnie has blabbed. Truth, at least, is dignified; I feel I have made enough of a fool of myself.

106

'I'm not,' I say, 'a bloke.'

'Well, you are almost . . . need to put on a bit of muscle, get rid of the squeaky voice. . . .'

I do not have a squeaky voice and I am furious.

'Come off it, Glyn. She's told you, hasn't she? Bit dumb of you not to spot it sooner though.'

'Told me what? And who's "she"?'

'Don't play the innocent with me. Jinnie, that's who. Your mum.'

'What's she supposed to have told me, then?'

I sigh with exasperation; this is going on too long.

'That I'm a girl, dope!'

There is a long silence. Then he shakes his head and grins.

'Diawl . . .! Who would have thought of it?'

I have had quite enough of this pantomime.

'Finish your ride,' I say curtly. 'Show's over!'

'Now wait a minute, Sam. I did think, yes, right from the start . . . but you played it so well that I could never be really sure. I even tried to trap you, shock some girlie reaction out of you – remember what I said about Louisa? – but you never let up. Don't expect me to be surprised because I'm not, but it was a bloody good act – see, even now I can't switch, I'm still calling you Sam. What's your real name?'

'Cealie.'

'I'll stick to Sam if you don't mind. So why the boy act?'

'The woman down at the shop started it—'

'Oh her? Not surprised – she's as thick as two bricks.'

'— and then Miss Matthias assumed it—'

'The hair, I suppose – not much of it, is there? Not

much of anything else, either, now I come to think of it.'

I pick up a dry crust and throw it at him.

'— so that leaves Gwen. Didn't she recognize you?'

'She hasn't seen me since I was a baby.'

'Aye-aye. Used her, then, did you?'

I suddenly feel like a bad smell. 'She was just there . . . at the right time. . . .' It does not sound convincing. I try to justify myself. 'I haven't actually done her any harm, you know. Your mum thinks I may even have done her some good.'

He takes a couple of cans of Coke from the cavernous pockets of his khaki jacket and tosses me one.

'Funny old thing, your auntie. . . . Remember her when I was a kid. Lived with her brother then; he had a job in a bank but when he got back here he used to fancy himself as a shepherd or something . . . used to go walking up here, oilskin cape, heavy boots, even a stick. Very strait-laced they were, always telling us off for something or other . . . lived in another age, Mam used to say. It's funny, but she's become a lot more interesting since she flipped.'

'Maybe,' I say, thinking it out, 'the daft bit was always there, waiting to jump out.'

'Or in her case, fly.'

'Like the boy bit, perhaps, was always inside me. . . .' I am impressing him, I can see that. Damn it, I am impressing myself.

'Clever stuff, man,' he teases. 'Psychological . . . way above my head. Things bad at home then? Presume that's why you're up here.'

'They seemed bad to me, though you probably wouldn't think so.'

108

'What I think doesn't really matter, though, does it? Your problem, isn't it? Nothing to do with me. . . . Going back sometime though?'

'Don't really know. To see them, yes. . . . I mean, you never really escape, do you?'

'I know what you mean. . . . I feel pretty desperate myself sometimes.'

'Up here?' I am amazed. 'When you can get out and ride for ever across these hills?'

'It's Mam, see. She's got this neat little plan all worked out for me . . . A levels, can't get anywhere without those, she says . . . then university; she always regretted not finishing her education. Aberystwyth, she fancies . . . sea air – good for me – and the Welsh language. Can't say I've given it much thought myself.' I am staggered by the bitterness in his voice. 'End up with some useless Arts degree and no job but I won't have to join the dole queue like the rest of them. . . . I've got Pentre all set up for me, see.'

'Pentre? What's that?'

'Never looked at the name of our house, then?' I have but my own pronounciation had been different. 'Pentre – the Stables, man; we've been building that business up for years; ate, drank, slept and shat those bloody horses since Dad walked out. Pony-struck kids who come drooling up here. Can't get away from them . . . another lot already booked in for this afternoon. That's why I came out – for a bit of privacy, for the luxury of my own thoughts.'

'And you got mine. I'm sorry.'

'Oh, you . . . you're neutral; you don't bother me. You don't load on the pressure, try to send me up; try to get off with me. Romantic Welsh horse-boy, it turns them on, see. You even have an uncommitted attitude to our four-legged friends and that's refreshing.'

He puts an arm on my shoulder.

'See, if you were really a bloke and I did this, just to show that I liked you, I'd be labelled gay. And if you were a girl, it would be Step One in one of their elaborate sexual games. You can't win, man. But you're just Sam and that's great.'

The touch of his hand does not exactly reinforce my status of sexual neutrality. If I am not very careful, I could get quite fond of him. . . .

'All gone yobbos!' he calls out comfortingly as he rides away. 'Got the hills to yourself again.'

I could go on but, remembering the uphill trek back through boggy ground, I feel unenthusiastic. Also there is Gwennie, sleeping off her cold. I feel I ought to be checking on her, taking her warm drinks and aspirins or something like that. Using her? I do not think I am. You have to see someone as an object if you want to do that, something to be shoved around and manipulated. Gwennie is a person. I am really quite fond of her.

I arrive back, footsore and breathless, to come eyeball to eyeball with Miss Matthias on the stairs. Her face is a thundercloud.

'I'm shocked,' she says, her tight lips snapping out the words. 'Thoroughly shocked.'

I am confused. 'By what?' I ask.

This seems to put her back up even more.

'Don't you be so insolent, young man. There's no caring with you youngsters, no respect.'

I do not attempt to defend my generation in my usual manner. Something is wrong. I am suddenly frightened. Is it Gwen?

'Is she worse?' I asked lamely.

'A fat lot you care! Leaving an old lady in that state, gallivanting out – some girl from down the Evanses, is it? Running a temperature, your Auntie, but I don't suppose you even noticed. I've notified the doctor of course,' she adds virtuously.

My own sardonic echo, 'Of course,' is quite lost on her but I do not care. Right now I am not feeling flippant.

'He'll be round sometime before six. Can't say when, exactly. Can't dictate to them,' she says reverently.

'No.' I am shaking. 'Can I go up?' I am asking her permission, like a child. She is clearly the one in charge here.

'Nothing to do now, is there? Sleeping peacefully; best leave her alone.'

'That's what she was doing when I left this morning,' I protest. It isn't fair, loading all the blame on to me.

'Not the point, though, is it? You don't leave old people alone in that state; you should have known better.'

'Well, what used to happen before I came?' I demand.

'What happened before is not relevant now, young man. You *are* here now. Sense of responsibility, see – though I can't say I'm surprised. Don't have much of that your lot. . . .'

'Who?'

'That precious family of yours. Sending you up here for a free holiday doing what you please; taking advantage of a poor old lady they can't be bothered to visit themselves. What's in it for them, then? Saves their consciences a bit, does it? If it's her money they're after – sending you up here to make a good impression on her – they won't see much of that, poor old thing.'

I am furious.

'They're both working! And it's a hell of a long way for them to come!'

'Up from Swansea? Tell me another, boyo. Got a car, I presume.'

'Look,' I say desperately, 'I'm fond of Auntie Gwen.'

'I don't doubt it for one minute,' she replies unexpectedly. 'Fond don't make responsibility, though; fond's not enough. And what kid would want to be cooped up here with a daft old woman anyway?'

'It hasn't been too bad.'

She pulls a nurse's watch out of her anorak pocket.

'I'd stay and wait for him but she's not the only one I ought to be seeing.'

'I am not,' I say firmly, 'going out again.' I mean it. No chance.

'Glad to hear it. I can count on you then. Be round tomorrow sometime. Any deterioration, let me know on the double. Don't want Death by Negligence on our hands, do we?'

She sees my reaction and her face immediately softens. Awkwardly she puts out her hand in what she intends to be a sympathetic gesture.

'No use trying to put an old head on young shoulders,' she says. 'You and I'll have to work together over the next few days until some kind of solution is found, so we'd better be friends. See, she doesn't want to be any trouble, our Gwennie, but look at the amount of trouble she's putting on

112

you. . . . Ought to be properly looked after at her time of life, but she won't listen. Stubborn as a mule, our Gwennie.'

The minute she leaves I run fearfully upstairs, expecting a corpse. Instead, I find her lying on her side, sleeping noisily, her face flushed and slimy and her hair lying in damp coils over her pink scalp. I leave her and go creeping around on tiptoe looking for distractions. Even the garden now feels out of bounds. Supposing she called out? Fell? Died?

I turned back to my book. Right now I have quite a desperate need for that glamour world of high budget films and lovesick but ambitious starlets. I am being turned on by the sensitive advances of the Man She Really Loves, when a car pulls up outside. An eager, intellectual type gets out. He is thin and energetic, with a clever smile – not at all the plump, comfortable family doctor I had imagined.

'You the grand-nephew, I presume. Didn't realize there were such things.'

I follow him docilely upstairs.

'Where's the rest of the family – got a sister still alive, hasn't she?'

Megan. My gran. 'Yes.'

'Got her address? Just in case . . .?'

I give it. Now I am well and truly cornered.

He pushes her over like a sack of potatoes and tucks a thermometer under her armpit.

'Can't trust her not to bite . . . some of them do.' He sounds like a vet.

She opens one eye.

'Go away,' she grumbles.

He raises his voice. 'It's Dr Williams, Miss Davies. You've got a bit of a chill.'

'Rubbish,' she says, and pulls the sheets up over her head.

'She shouldn't be left,' he instructs me as we walk downstairs. 'Miss Matthias told me you'd been out most of the day – well, we can't have that sort of thing right now. A bit young for this much responsibility, aren't you?'

'I'm sixteen.'

'Don't look it.'

'I can cope.'

He takes a bottle of pale green pellets out of his bag and counts out half a dozen into the palm of his hand.

'Antibiotics,' he explains. 'One every four hours, if you can manage to get them down her. I'll be around in the morning to take another look at her. And for goodness sake don't leave the house without letting someone know – old people in that state can easily get pneumonia.'

12

There is a nightmarish feeling about the house this evening. I have, with incredible difficulty, conned Gwen into swallowing a green pill and she has been asleep for some time. As dusk grows, I switch on the light for reassurance and settle down uneasily to finish my paperback. The final embrace is really quite something. The knock on the door wrenches me brusquely out of the hero's arms.

The face at the window is just the one I need: it is Jinnie. I let her in gratefully.

'How's the old lady?'

'How did you know?'

She laughs at this.

'Try keeping anything a secret in Bettws for more than a couple of hours. . . . Mouse farts in the next valley and they hear it down the Drovers' Arms. Getting yourself a bit of a bad press, Sam, you know, and don't say I didn't warn you.'

I groan. 'The Matthias?'

'Who else?'

'I'm only staying here,' I say indignantly. 'I'm not her nurse – and anyway, how was I to know?'

'Calm down, bach – we all know that. . . . But you've landed yourself with a tricky situation, you know, and all this old fibbing don't help things.'

'I told Glyn,' I say quickly.

'I know. He mentioned it. . . . Look, Sam, make us a pot of tea, and maybe, between us, we can sort out some of the mess.'

She follows me into the kitchen and sits down at the table.

'Brought you some chocolate digestives,' she says, opening a packet. 'Always comforting in times of stress, I find. Now look, boyo, Sam, Cealie, whatever you are, you've got to come clean – at least with your family, because you're going to need them if things get bad.'

I feel trapped but I cannot disagree.

'Now why don't you and I get together and do it this way . . . tell a few white lies of our own to cover up your whoppers. Day after tomorrow I've got to go down to Swansea on business . . . now why don't you ring your mam and tell her I'm popping in; you can say that you've got a holiday job up at Pentre and you've gone to see your auntie. I'll tell her auntie's a bit poorly and have a word with her about the "boy" thing so you'll be more or less covered. She'll probably just laugh it off, she'll be so relieved to know where you are. Then they can come up here in their own time and you can all sort things out between you. If the old lady gets any worse, they'd want to be involved anyway, wouldn't they? And if they need a bed for a night or two I could always put them up in the spare bedroom if they're prepared to take pot luck. How about that?'

Horrified, I mumble, 'Great.'

She takes a small notebook out of her bag.

'Let's have your address then.'

116

And I tell her.

Jinnie is amazing.

'London now, is it? What next?' No big drama, no fuss, nothing more than mild surprise and a new aspect of the problem to be dealt with. Load that little bundle of deceptions on to Mum and after the hysterics she would be trying to psychoanalyze me.

'Hitched with a couple of friends down to Porthcawl . . . thought I'd find myself a summer job but it didn't work out so I came up here.'

'And how does Gwennie fit into all this?'

'She is really my great-aunt; I knew she lived in this place called Bettws. It's my gran who lives in Swansea.'

Jinnie ponders for a while, working it all out. The silence is very peaceful.

'Not much point in me bothering your gran, is there?' She says at last. 'Give her a fright and probably all for nothing. No reason why your auntie shouldn't pull through this one . . . won't be the first time she's had us all jumping. She may be a bit cuckoo by anyone else's standards but she's as tough as old boots, I'll say that for her.'

The next morning I am not at all sure about that statement.

For one thing, she will neither eat nor drink, so how can I give her a pill? For another, she is talking nonsense: real nonsense this time, not just phrases out of line.

I go in to her with buttered bread, a cup of tea, a glass of water and a green pill, all nicely arranged on one of her scratched tin trays. She glares at me out of moist blue eyes.

'Messing about in the kitchen again?' she

117

grumbles. 'Won't have you untidying my things, John – takes me a week to clear up after you've been in there.' She struggles to get out of bed but I push her back against the pillows.

'It's me, Auntie Gwen. Sam. Look.'

'Sam? Don't know no Sam. Who's Sam, then, when he's at home?'

'I've brought you your medicine.' I hold out the small, bullet-shaped pill and the glass of water. Last night it had been difficult. Now it was impossible. 'Don't want your old medicine . . . anyone would think I was an invalid,' and she buttons up her mouth like a stubborn toddler.

I try something else.

'Tea, then, Auntie,' pouring a little into the saucer for her. I am considering popping the pill in between mouthfuls but she is ahead of me, slippery as an eel.

'Don't want your old tea neither.'

She hauls the sheet up around her ears; her eyes are closed, but she is not sleeping.

'Don't want your old charity,' she mutters fiercely. 'Children of Satan, the whole lot of you . . . Sodom and Gomorrah with your tellies and your old sex . . . dirty . . . don't think I haven't seen you carrying on up there in the ferns. Daft Gwennie got eyes in her head like everyone else, hasn't she? Even on the Lord's Day . . . disgusting I call it but you won't listen, none of you listen, and Judgement Day is coming. . . .'

Under different circumstances this little monologue would just be a giggle but right now I am not amused. Fascinated, yes. I could almost suspect a performance laid on for my benefit if I didn't know better. I eat the bread myself – what else can I do? I

am hungry; I would prefer my own breakfast downstairs but I dare not leave her.

'Just like animals . . . even her, my own little niece
. . . you'd have thought Megan would've drummed
some sense into her. . . . Knew where to come to in
the end though, didn't they? No Daft Gwennie for
you then, just "Gwen, help us out" . . . and I did. . . .
Had more pride myself . . . wouldn't let Edward lay a
finger on me. . . . All that love sacrificed to your old
age. . . .'

She opens her eyes and stares right through me.

'Not that I regret it for one minute, mind. . . . I did
my duty, more than you can say for Megan . . . right
up to the end, you can't deny that.'

'Of course you did,' I say firmly. 'No doubt about
it.'

She is restless now and very hot. Her mouth is
loose and open but I dare not push in a pill in case she
chokes. My ears are straining for the sound of the
doctor's car, but all I can hear is the soft sweep-sweep
of fine rain across the windows and the occasional
twitter of a bird.

In a plaintive treble, very off-key, she begins to
sing.

'What – a friend we have in – Je – sus . . .'

The singing seems to bring about a change in
mood.

'I've reaped my reward a thousandfold. . . .
Shining bright you are, my angel . . . wings as white
as swan's and a glory in your face . . . there's
beautiful you are and you're all mine . . . nobody else
has got you. . . .'

She is sweating profusely. I dip the corner of the
sheet in the glass of water and bathe her forehead.

'There's kind you are,' she says, suddenly rational. Then, pulling my face down towards her, she whispers in my ear: 'You ought to meet my little niece . . . fancy her, you would . . . about your age, my Winnie . . . spends all her time up there drawing pictures . . . just like a little child.' She winks at me. 'Nice boy like you . . . might make her act her age for once.'

All at once her face crumples.

'Rivers of tears she cried, rivers of tears; won't she ever stop crying? Stop her, John, tell her to stop . . . find something to do, then – slap her face, why don't you? All over now and no one even laid a finger on her . . . lucky little girl right back where she started and no one any the wiser. . . . God's way's the best way but why won't she let me touch her. . .?"

The doctor walks into the middle of all this. I have not even heard the car.

'What's all this, then? Storm in a tea-cup? Calm yourself, there's a good girl; you're not doing yourself one bit of good by it, you know.'

'. . . but she won't stop crying . . .'

'There now: listen. She's stopped – no more crying. Can you hear anyone crying, Sam?' He turns to me. 'How long has she been like this?'

'Only a few minutes. But she's been saying a lot of silly stuff for quite some time.'

He tucks the thermometer under her arm and fingers her limp wrist.

'I'm not surprised. . . . She's a pretty sick lady. How about the pills?'

'I gave her two yesterday evening but she wouldn't take one this morning.'

'What's this I hear?' He scolds her as if she is a

120

naughty kid. 'Not taking your medicine? There's a bad girl you are. Open now: no nonsense – good. Now a mouthful of this to wash it down. . . .'

When we go downstairs, Miss Matthias is already tapping at the window to be let in. Tiptoeing heavily, she follows the doctor back to Gwen's room, carefully maintaining a respectful distance. Their voices are low but by listening carefully I can pick up snatches of their conversation.

'. . . much too young for this kind of responsibility . . . and where's the family, that's what I'd like to know . . .'

'. . . check the Cottage Hospital . . . might be able to get her admitted this afternoon . . . emergency after all . . . needs proper nursing . . .'

I am offended by all this. I mean – under the circumstances I have not done too badly.

'Sam.' The Matthias tries on a firm but kindly voice but I am not impressed. 'You do realize, don't you, that your auntie is very sick?' What does she take me for – an imbecile? 'Dr Williams is going to try to get her into hospital as soon as possible, maybe even today. One or other of us will let you know what's happening but while it's being sorted out, we want your word of honour that you won't leave the house.'

I am livid.

'You do not,' I inform her icily, 'have to tell me.'

That, damn it, gives her the perfect opening.

'I did,' she reminds me smugly, 'yesterday.'

Sensing my antagonism, Dr Williams smooths things over with: 'Hold the fort, Sam. Be a brave chap – we're counting on you. Shouldn't be for long.'

After they leave, I wander around in silence,

looking for things to do. I collect the breakfast things, the sticky plate and the half-drunk tea with its milky moonskin floating thin and cold on its surface, and hurry away from the heavy-breathing hump on the bed. I am scared of her now. I do not want to go near her. She's no longer Gwennie, she's something else and I do not want to know.

Go on. Say it: it is all my fault, isn't it? But it wasn't me who conjured up the vision in the apple tree. I didn't lace her tea with grass and entice her into the rain with fancy tales about an angel. But I know what they're saying about me – not that I care. '. . . callously abandoning a sick old lady . . . goes off tramping over the hills regardless. . . .' I might tell it differently but who, apart from the Evanses, is going to believe a yarn spun by a boy or was it a girl, the product of some dubious family in Swansea, whose motives for sending him to Bettws in the first place are extremely suspect?

I hate myself. I wish I was dead. It's not the first time I've wished that; imagined the ripple of shock that would run through my class. Cealie Thomson? Dead? Killed herself? Wow . . . That would get them – Princess Daisy done something real at last. Trouble is, of course, I wouldn't be around to take the credit.

Time drags on. I long for something normal like the sound of a telephone ringing – even a wrong number would mean that there was someone else in the world besides me. I cook myself an omelette but I have no appetite. No telephone, no television . . . telly would be wonderful; right now I could watch anything, even the test card. There is always the Magic Box upstairs of course, with its possibilities of more steamy revelations, but I do not feel in the mood.

Rituals around Going Into Hospital stir in my memory. I mean, you have to have a clean dressing gown and slippers, don't you, and a nicely packed toilet bag. The toilet bag takes the longest; I become almost obsessive about it, rummaging through her chaos until, finally, I unearth two. I even manage to dig out one of those gift boxes with soap and bath cubes and talcum powder, so that, later, when Miss Matthias arrives in a small ambulance, everything is packed and ready.

Predictably she ignores me, dancing attendance on the two stretcher bearers as they go upstairs. I would only be in the way. As they bring her down, I can hear Gwennie coughing and protesting. It is only then that Miss Matthias chooses to acknowledge my efforts.

'There's a thoughtful boy you are, Sam,' she says, sweeping it all together.

We form a little procession, across the front garden and into the road. Under the dripping hedge a group of urchins has gathered to watch the fun.

Gwen spots them at once.

'Making a spectacle out of me for no reason at all,' she grumbles, and raising her voice she calls out weakly, 'Got no homes to go to then?' The kids snigger but do not move.

Her eyes suddenly light on me.

'Sam,' she says wearily, 'where am I going then?'

'To hospital, Auntie Gwen, but only for a few days.'

'No trick, is it, to get me into a Home?'

'No trick.'

'You'd tell me the truth, Sam?'

'Course I would.'

'And who's going to look after things while I'm gone?'

'Don't you go worrying your head over things like that,' begins Miss Matthias, but I put in quickly: 'I will.'

'That's a good boy . . . mind you lock up properly . . . don't know who's hanging about these days.'

'Alright.'

'And close all the windows at night . . . air's bad for you . . .'

Rounding the corner, they have gone.

The sky is all patchwork cloud, its glittering seams blown ragged by the wind. I lock up the house.

It is a relief to run, pumping my legs like a piston, flailing my arms and feeling the chilly air race past my shorn head. I slam into the telephone box and dial my own number. It is nearly five and I hope someone will be there. Even my mother. This time I really need them.

'Roz?'

'That Cealie?'

'Yes.'

'Mum's out.'

'Oh.' There is a frigid silence, an icy full stop to this conversation. It is abundantly clear that she does not wish to speak to me.

'Roz. . .' I have to prevent her from ringing off. 'Want my address.'

'Not particularly.'

'Look, I've got a problem—'

At this she explodes.

'You've got a problem? Well, poor old you – what about the rest of us?'

124

'Look, I'm sorry . . .'

'Sorry? That's a joke. You, I suppose, are having a lot of fun, wherever you are. We had to cancel our two weeks in France because of you and I don't suppose you give a damn! You're just a selfish pig, Cealie, and I don't want to speak to you!'

'But Roz—'

'Don't "But Roz" me. . . . Any idea of the state Mum's been in? Do you even care?' She straightaway answers for me. 'No, you do not. The only person you care about is your fat self, so stuff your problem!'

'If you give her my address it might make her feel better.'

'Give it to her yourself!'

Contact, if it had ever been established, is now shattered.

I stand looking at the buzzing telephone in my hand, not quite believing it. Roz – damn you – I needed you and you wouldn't even listen. . . .

I need someone. I need someone right now. I could try later, speak to Mum, but that isn't good enough. The Evanses are away for the day and who the hell else is there?

I suddenly think of my dad: quiet, vague, detached and unemotional. For the first time in my life he is precisely what I need.

I ring the bookshop.

'Mr Thomson? Hold one moment, please. . . .'

I hold, grimly, listening to the pips and counting my diminishing store of change. He comes at last.

'Owls Bookshop. Colin Thomson here – can I help you?'

'Yes, you can, Dad. It's Cealie.'

'Good God!'

'Listen, Dad. I'm living with Auntie Gwen at Bettws.'

'Who the hell is Auntie Gwen?'

'Mum's Auntie Gwen – the one in the Black Mountains.'

'Good God!'

'Is that all you can say?' I snap.

'Well. . . I suppose you want to be picked up,' he says, as if I had been staying late at Ranjit's.

'Not yet. . . I mean, I don't know. Look, she's been taken ill. She's actually in hospital and I'm holding the fort until something happens, one way or the other – will you tell Mum?'

'Dramatic stuff,' he says vaguely. There is a short silence, out of which comes the totally unexpected. 'I'm impressed,' he says. 'Brave girlie.'

I push it away with a 'Not really, just got stuck with it', but actually I am pleased. My dad never flatters. In fact, I think he finds it quite difficult to say nice things to people, even his own family.

'What about money?'

Mine has just run out.

'I'll ring tomorrow.' I just manage to get in, 'Love to Mum . . . and Roz . . .' before the line goes dead.

I stop off at the village shop for a few basics – eggs, chocolate, two bananas and some coffee. The red-haired woman is nowhere to be seen; there is only the man who usually works in the Post Office. I have never really looked at him before and I do not like what I see now – a beefy, overstuffed face, lecherous eyes and dark hair furrowed with grease. He moves sluggishly, putting things together with irritating deliberation as if he has to work it all out again for me.

'Hear the old lady's been taken bad?'

It is a question, not a statement. I have no great desire to feed his curiosity.

'She's in hospital,' I say briefly.

'Hospital now, is it?' His right eyelid droops in a toadlike wink. 'Been giving her a hard time then, have you?'

That hurts, even coming from him.

'What the hell do you mean by that?'

'Language, language . . .' His little barb had unexpectedly drawn blood and he is obviously quite pleased with himself.

'Been beating her up, have you?'

'You're crazy!'

'Not as crazy as a daft old woman all alone who lets a total stranger into her house, some kid from nowhere. Beat 'em up for a farthing, some of you lot . . . not saying you're like that mind . . . just my little joke, see.'

I feel sick.

'I am her nephew, you know,' I say, not wanting to offer him even that piece of information.

'Nephew or niece, is it? Butcher thought you was a girl. Twenty pence change – now don't look at me like that: I was only teasing.'

I get out of there in a hurry. I want to kill him. If his rotten display of fake Swiss Army knives had been out on the counter, I might have.

13

The sight of the empty house gives me the creeps, so I dump the cardboard box so lovingly packed by the plump pink hands of the man in the shop and run out on to the hills. I feel dirty; I need the purification of all those silvered clouds and the peppermint prickle of rain and the gusty wind which takes my breath away. A kind of rage races me over ground through which I had cautiously picked only a few days ago, and brings me, muddy and drenched, to the edge of the forestry plantation.

I step with misgivings into a black witches' forest. I have never come so far before. The last of the light flicks over the wiry tangle of thin branches at the base of the trees and then I find myself walking in a lovat-green twilight. The narrow, bone-white path – a space left between ruler-straight plantings – seems like the magic path that I must follow. Silly, but why not? It is dead straight so I cannot get lost.

Small, unfamiliar sounds are woven through the silence: the constant drip-drip of moisture through the trees, the small thud of a falling cone, a sudden upward flutter of an unseen bird. Pine needles slither and scutter under my feet and even my breath smells resinous. I walk until light shows at the end of the path. Then I walk into the light.

Mole-like and blinking, I find myself on the bright shores of the reservoir, my magical lake of shining waters. A fringe of ferns, flattened by rain, fans out over grey and pink stones. I flop down, dazed by the light, my legs aching after my long walk. Over the opposite shoreline, the cloud shadows play hide and seek over terracotta and green and gold, the colours glowing and fading, and below me the water clinks, and winks a thousand evil jade eyes.

I walk down to the lake's edge to soak the mud from the legs of my jeans. The water beckons and dances. There is a noticeboard: DEEP WATER. SWIMMING STRICTLY PROHIBITED. So what? I strip down to bra and pants and slide shiveringly into it. I am not a bad swimmer and I am not worried. Lying on my back I attempt to float on its choppy surface, splashing around with my arms and legs. This feels good.

But the sky thickens and the light becomes cold and I want out: I have had enough. But this is not like a pool or a friendly sea-shore. Spray spangles the nicotine-yellow clouds as the sharp waves slap into my face. Somehow I have drifted. This is what you get for trespassing in a forbidden lake. The freezing water boils up around me; I am simmering in a cauldron of ice.

Desperately I lunge out for the shore but an army of cut-glass springs up all around me. The sun is a yellow pearl rolled up in gauze. I swallow water and shiver. So this is Death, then – relentless, cold, strong and irresistible. No angel's wings for Cealie but then Cealie is a bad girl, broke her mother's heart and killed poor old Gwennie . . . Cealie is a slag . . . sleeps

129

around at parties. . . . Accusations are scrawled all glittery over the liquid valleys and hills and they are all true . . . guilty . . . guilty . . . no point in struggling any more; relax, let the water take you. . . .

My fingers open and close around something solid – a bone? his wrist? I pull it towards me . . . sharp little twigs scratch against my skin.

My watch, waterlogged, has stopped. Time has stopped.

I cannot remember for how long I have been lying here, dripping, slumped over the pebbles and rocks, staining them dark with my body. I passed out. I dreamed.

Now, with evening, the sky is clear, its glassy blue warmed by the beginning of a sunset. Dry and surprisingly warm, I dress and begin walking back through the gloom of the forest, no thoughts in my head now, not even fear; simply a gnawing hunger. I wonder if there is any bread left – I forgot to buy any. And I spend a long time considering the flavour of bananas and the taste of chocolate. . . .

Grateful now to be back, I roll my legs over the stone wall and walk round to the front to unlock the door. Glyn, squatting on the step, looks up from his book.

''lo, Sam. You took long enough. Where you been then?'

'Trying to drown myself in the reservoir,' I reply flippantly. I feel a mess.

'Bad place to go swimming, down there . . . you want to be careful.'

He points out a basket full of bulging bags, a treacle tart covered in cling film and a bottle of cider.

'Been doing your shopping?'

He shakes his head.

'Supper,' he says. 'Listen, let us in, will you? Been waiting out here for ages, man.'

He sets the basket down on the kitchen table and brings out of it some apples, a couple of pork pies, a fresh green salad in a yellow plastic box and a couple of potatoes baked in silver foil.

'Matthias called in . . . more concerned about you than Gwennie.'

'Really? Didn't seem that way this morning.'

'She's going to be alright, your auntie, by the way; called in earlier to let you know but you weren't there. We'd only just got back when she caught us – well, you know Matthias – had to have the whole story down to every last detail. Mam's idea, the supper. Felt sorry for you. Got a soft spot for you, Mam. . . .'

I look at the bottle of cider.

'She think I'm a lush? That's a hell of a lot for one person.'

'What about me then? Go on – let's have some plates.'

Light-headed already on a teacupful of cider, I set out the pantry collection of cracked and mismatched plates with all the formality of a child playing at house.

'It was fantastic of Jinnie to dream up all this . . .'

It's beginning to feel like a clowns' dinner-party. We set out the salad with spoons and forks and balance the treacle tart in its foil container on a tarnished silver cake-stand we have found in a cupboard. We even stuff two candle stubs into egg-cups and light them.

131

Glyn pours some more cider.

'Cheers,' he says. 'There's posh we are.'

Lately, at home, I have been feeling terribly self-conscious at dinner-parties, as if the act of eating, performed by me, was vaguely disgusting. Traces of this feeling return to me now when he says: 'London now is it? Swansea not good enough for you, then? Where next?' and then, fooling, suddenly 'boy-with-girl': 'What's Bettws got that Piccadilly hasn't? Spare my modesty now. . . .'

He picks up my reaction and puts things right.

'Sorry, Sam. Bloody silly sort of thing to say to you.' The relaxed and easy friendship between us is at once restored.

I look at his smooth, young face, more boy than man, cheeks rosed and freckled by the sun (not my type at all: I go for dark, languid blokes like Bill who wear trendy clothes and look experienced) and remember Gareth the Womanizer. 'He can touch me anywhere. . . .' How naive girls were then, I think, but for some reason, I shiver.

'What's your dad like?' I ask, in order to distract myself.

He immediately resents the question.

'A man,' he said tersely. Then he relents. 'He's alright, I suppose . . . took us all out to tea this afternoon. We're a nice little family, see, if you put us all together once a month, preferably in a public place; more than that and it's bloody murder, man. How about yours?'

'Relatively peaceful.' But stagnant, I think. Stagnant and deep. You could drown in the quiet waters of my family and no one would hear you scream.

'Head full of fancies, my dad . . . dreams and

fancies; never grew up properly, Mam says. She runs the whole show, really, or likes to think she does. Gets under her skin good and proper me wanting to act . . . thinks I'll end up like him. Makes her think she's a failure, see, if she hasn't got a finger in every pie.'

He has been playing with the apples on the plate. Suddenly, throwing one of them up in the air, he begins, very expertly, to juggle with all four. I watch in amazement.

'That's impressive!'

'Don't impress her . . . juggling don't run stables or land me a good job at a bank. Just like my dad. . . .'

'Is that so bad?'

'Not brilliant. Freelance reporter for some left-wing newspaper . . . at his age. I mean that's all he does. Oh, he does the odd bit in the nationals once in a blue moon . . . reads poetry – his own stuff, mostly – in pubs, and just about breaks even. Girlfriend supports them most of the time I suspect . . . until she gets wise and walks out on him – they all do, see. That's how it was with Mam until she sussed him out . . . couldn't take any more, see. Still fancies her. Strong women turn him on, I think.'

The bitterness in his voice is quite unbearable; I quickly change the subject.

'My problem's just the opposite . . .'

The shadows deepen. Outside, the night is luminous, the sky reluctant to cast off the warm embers of sunset. Invisible wings rustle against the pale stars and an owl calls from the trees.

'Swap you London any day.'

I laugh at this one. 'Oh, yes, all those things it means if you don't actually live there . . . theatres, galleries, night-clubs.'

133

'Oh no, not my scene at all. Buskers, street theatre, that's where it's at for me, not those old museums and things. Give me that piazza place in Covent Garden or the guys in the underground any day. Try to do that sort of thing down here and they think you've gone mad. . . . I want to give it a try though, see. I've got this idea for a sort of modern Mari Lwyd—'

'A Mari what?'

'Mari Lwyd. Mummers, mime . . . old custom round here once. We've got this crackpot idea of reviving it, bringing it right into the Nineties, making it into some kind of political satire, that sort of thing.'

'We?'

'A couple of like-minded nutcases.'

'In Welsh?'

'Possibly that too. Why not?'

'Pity. . . .'

'Why?'

'No bit parts for me.'

'We just might consider using a civilized foreigner.'

We are both a bit tipsy now, drunk more on the interaction between us than the cider: high as the moon.

We stay up until well past midnight. I mean, he is so easy to talk to. Conversation grows like a flower, flourishes. We slice our mothers in half and join them down the middle to create a perfect parent and then decide that there is really no such thing. We even marry Roz off to David – same types, really: snotty little family babies with an overdose of self-confidence.

Between us we re-design the world. I mean, anything is possible. . . .

134

Next morning I open my eyes on nursery brightness and a cloudless sky and come down to a letter. I
am amazed to find it addressed to Miss Cealie
Thomson and postmarked London – must have
baffled the postman. The sun has drawn slanting
rectangles over the kitchen walls. I pour myself a cup
of coffee, butter some bread and open up the
envelope. Four fivers, swaying like kites, fall out of
the single fold of paper. I read the letter. It is very
brief.

'Thought these might help. Got your address
(Aunt Gwen's) from Mummy. We await further
instructions. In haste – lots of love, Dad.'

No accusations, no awkward questions – for once I
respond with gratitude to the abstract presence of my
vague, unemotional dad. Mum would want the
inside story right away and feel rejected if she didn't
get one, but what is there to tell? I don't know. . . .
Checking the apple tree for supernatural presences
– and on this shining morning anything is possible – I
prop one of the kitchen chairs among the campion
and dock and stretch out in the sun.
I try not to think about Glyn. I think about Mum
instead. Why, for instance, do her faintly 'arty'
clothes embarrass me so much? They don't seem to
bother Roz. And why do I keep seeing myself in some
chocolate-box picture, one of her Victorian things:
Freda Thomson and Her Two Lovely Children? I do
not want to be anyone's lovely child; I just want to be
like everyone else.
A car pulls up in the road outside and jolts me out
of my sun-drowse. Someone tries the front door and

dances fingers across the windowpane.

'Sam?'

I yawn indolently and walk across to her.

'Oh, there you are. . . . I'm going in to see how Auntie is. Want to come with me?'

Dressed up for hospital visiting in straw hat and violet Crimplene, Miss Matthias is clutching a small box of jellied fruit. 'Can't go in empty-handed.'

Cashing in on my sudden affluence, I pick up a fiver before I leave.

The old leather briefcase on the passenger seat is dumped into the dough of cushions in the back. The sheepskin covers have a sweet scent. I wind the window all the way down. As we move off, she attacks me brightly with: 'Mam not coming up today then? Wouldn't want to intrude on family. . . .'

'She can't make it today.'

'I should hope tomorrow then. Can't leave you up here coping all by yourself – it's not right. Auntie'd feel happier too. Nothing like your own flesh and blood around you when you're in that state.'

'I thought she was better.'

'Yes, but there's no telling,' she hints darkly, 'at that age.'

I glance sideways at her stout, cheerful figure and think: what power she wields, even over me. There is nothing I want less than to have my parents in this place but one or both of them will have to come or Gwen will never hear the end of it.

'Could we stop off at a flower shop?' I ask.

'No need for that, Sam – flower stall at the hospital.'

But that is not what I want. Feeling guilty still, I am vaguely looking for something special, and my

136

eyes go skimming over the predictable shops at Llanharan until I spot it: CHARLOTTE ROSE: SAY IT WITH FLOWERS, tucked, coy as a bridesmaid, between Jones the Ironmongers and the Principality Building Society.

'There,' I say. 'Please stop.'

'Cheaper at the hospital; pay a premium in these little shops,' she grumbles, but she parks just the same.

I look over roses, gladioli, lilies and early chrysanthemums but come out with a gold-ribboned orchid in a cellophane box.

Miss Matthias is astounded. I am pretty surprised myself.

'What's that when it's at home?'

'An orchid.'

'Funny thing to bring someone in hospital.' Aware, suddenly, of the unkindness of this, she tries to cover it up. 'Don't see very many of those around. It's very nice. Don't you listen to me . . . only hope she appreciates it.'

St Asaph's Cottage Hospital is no cottage. We follow a maze of signposts to Grace Ward with no trouble at all; Miss Matthias has been here so often she could drive it blindfold, she tells me.

Grace Ward is one of a series of outbuildings connected to the main block by a long corridor.

The Sister's voice is soft as fleece.

'Hullo, Miss Matthias, there's nice to see you. She's better today, sitting up and taking notice. Soon have her back on your hands again. She hasn't been moved; down there – last bed but one.'

'This is her nephew, Sam.'

'Oh yes. . . .'

Her disbelieving frown follows me as I pick my way between the beds, watched by the curious or uncomprehending eyes of the geriatric ward where the smell of fresh flowers does not quite conceal the odour of stale urine and where a radio dimly bleats out the inanities of a chat show to which no one is listening.

She is propped up on pillows looking dead again. Miss Matthias utters the magic formula.

'Gwen? I've brought your young man.'

Her eyelids flick open.

'Sam. . . .' She stops herself from waxing too enthusiastic. 'Didn't expect to see you here. Miss Matthias brought you, did she? There's kind. Locked up properly, did you?'

I offer her my ribboned box. She is baffled.

'What's this then?'

'An orchid.'

'An orchid?' She turns the box round and round in her hands.

'Brought you some sweets, Gwen.' Miss Matthias plants the box firmly on the locker. 'Don't eat them all in one go.'

'Orchid . . . it's not a real one. . . .'

'Oh, yes.'

'Not plastic?'

'No.'

'Shouldn't have wasted your money. Orchid . . . we used to pin them to our dresses, going dancing . . . young man brought you an orchid it was something special . . .'

For once in her life, Miss Matthias says the right thing. It isn't just right: it is perfect.

'Well, now a young man has.'

138

Trouble is, I'm a fake. . . .

'Sam, I'd like a word with your parents when they turn up,' Miss Matthias announces on the way back. 'No problem about that, is there?'

'Oh no.' What else can I say?

'I'm retiring next spring, see,' she confides. 'Never properly professional anyway . . . just an old busy-body. All getting a bit too much for me these days . . . have to put Gwen on the Social Services over Tregaron. Whole bunch of enthusiastic youngsters over there and properly qualified too, not like me. Been running my own show for years. . . . Always offered, see, and then you can't let people down.'

There is no mistaking that tone of regret. What next for her, I wonder? A lifetime of living through other people's problems and now she has to come face to face with her own.

'What will you do?'

'Do?' At first the question seems to throw her off balance. 'Do?' She is almost offended. Then she gets it together. 'Well, I've got a bit of money stowed away . . . Thought I might move down to the seaside, Porthcawl, perhaps; take in summer visitors. Meet lots of nice people doing that . . . be a holiday in itself, not having anyone dependent on me any more.'

But her enthusiasm sounds fakey to me and there is a sort of sadness in her voice.

'Known her for donkey's years, old Gwen. Time she was properly cared for now – that's what I want to talk to your mam about.'

'But Mum can't do anything – it's up to Gwen, isn't it?'

'Not always, Sam. Think now: what if you hadn't been there that day. . .?'

'But you were.'

'I'm not there every day, though. She gets a bit of the special treatment because I'm living here in Bettws and I'm involved. New people'll work through their timetable, do what they're told; they won't be here on her doorstep each time she has a hiccup; they won't be around to pick her up when she goes off preaching to the ungodly.'

She sighs.

'Beautiful thought, the orchid. You're the romantic type, Sam. She'll be a lucky girl, whoever she is.'

I cannot keep it up any longer.

'Miss Matthias—'

'Going to tell me her name?'

'I'm not a boy, Miss Matthias. I just pretended.'

'What's all this nonsense?'

'I'm her grand-niece,' I announce desperately. 'From London. Her sister Megan's grand-daughter.' There is a shocked silence. 'Please believe me,' I beg, 'because it's true.' But why should she?

The silence lasts until we park outside the cottage. There she shows me the hurt in her pink, solid face.

'All a tissue of lies then, is it?'

'Look,' I snap. 'I had a row with my parents and I ran away. I hitched down here to stay with my gran in Swansea and then I thought of Auntie Gwen. More . . . anonymous up here.' It isn't quite the truth but it's close enough and it sounds good. 'Wasn't easy to tell you actually.' I am embarrassingly close to tears. 'I could have gone on pretending.'

'Sister wasn't taken in. And I have heard talk, mind: never listened to it, of course . . . believed the evidence of my own eyes, didn't I? Can't even do that these days.'

140

I do not know what to say to her.

'Winnie or Nancy?' she suddenly asks.

For a minute, I am baffled.

'Your Mam . . . which daughter?'

'Winnie.'

'Diawl. That takes me back . . . knew her when she was just a girl, used to come up here a lot. So that's who you are.'

'That's right.'

All at once, she laughs.

'Took us all in, me more than any of them. Daft Doris, they should call me.'

'I didn't mean any harm.'

'What's your real name, then? What did she call you?'

'Cealie . . . Cecilia.'

'There's a pretty name. Fancy you changing it for plain old Sam. Knew a Sam once, cross-eyed and snotty-nosed.'

'You won't tell Gwennie?' I ask nervously. I mean, honesty is OK as long as it doesn't hurt people.

She thinks about it.

'Spoil things for her a bit . . . take the gilt off the gingerbread, wouldn't it – her young man turning out to be a girl. How about your family though?'

'I'll sort them out,' I say firmly.

'Then my lips,' she declares solemnly, 'will be sealed.' Do you know, I do not think that anyone has ever shared a secret with her before. I mean, her eyes are all shiny; I think she is quite flattered.

It seems as if I have given her a present, too.

Listen, I am not so bad. In fact, right now I quite like myself. And it may sound silly to you, but if I were still a virgin I could almost believe that I was Gwennie's angel. . . .

14

I have to involve them now; I have to ring them but I don't want to.

The very idea of having my family here in Bettws makes me shudder. What a travelling circus! Clowns on both sides of the ring and a spotlight playing on the freak of the show. Me.

But there is another, darker side to their coming. Call it what you will – bad vibes or just my own fantasies – but I cannot be sure that Mum won't be affected by the ghost of that girl whose fragmented, passionate existence I have by chance uncovered. I do not have to show her the stuff, I know, but it is still there, ticking away like a time bomb.

I've got to make that call.

En route to the telephone, playing for time, I take a detour to the Evanses. There is always Glyn . . .

I have to admit that if I did not regard him as a sort of brother (I would swap Roz for him any day) I might even fancy Glyn. Hell, that would mess things up; I mean, I have never had such a good friendship with anyone before. I feel so relaxed with him and I wouldn't want sex to spoil things. No danger of that, though; the night he came to supper I was stinking of waterweed and about as laid back as a half-drowned puppy. The notion of playing the big seduction scene with Glyn is just a joke.

The dogs know me by heart and greet me like a member of the family. The yard is noisy with people and horses – the rough-coated hill ponies stamping and switching their tails; the people, all strangers, another new lot. Glyn is sorting out saddling problems for this useless looking female with streaked blonde curls. Some day, just for laughs, I must show him my little souvenir – my shorn-off tresses in their plastic bag, much more spectacular than hers. . . .

But now I need to speak to him. Only for a moment. I need some moral support – can't he see that?

A middle-aged couple are flapping and fussing over their kid. I hang around the edges of the group feeling small and silly, waiting to be noticed. At last he picks up my presence but he just says, ''lo, Sam,' and nothing else, as if the closeness we had shared only a couple of nights ago had never existed. So what? I am about to give up when I spot Jinnie standing by the kitchen door.

I need someone. Anyone.

'Hullo, Sam. Another lot today. Glyn and David've got their hands full this time. Come to keep me company then? Want a drop of tea? How's the old lady? Better?'

I sit next to her in the cool, sun-bronzed kitchen. The warm drink slips comfortingly down my throat.

I give her my problem.

'I've got to ring my family.'

'Good girl. Do it from here if you like – no trouble at all.'

'Lots of trouble . . . I mean, I haven't told them

properly about Gwen yet. They'll be down; might even be on their way now.'

'Only natural, Sam.'

'Well, I don't want it . . . and if my mother comes here it'll be a disaster.'

'That's a bit over the top, isn't it? Inconvenient, yes; a disaster, no.'

'I said a disaster and I mean it.' I have no intention of going into details and I certainly won't involve Jinnie in all that nonsense about Gareth. 'Someone will have to come, though . . . Miss Matthias already thinks we're negligent and I don't want people down here going on about her peculiar family – it would really upset her.'

'There's all that boy nonsense of yours, too.'

'That too. . . .'

'What about your dad?'

'What about him?'

'Well, what if he came, without her?'

I think about it.

'I could cope with that. You see, Mum'd weep all over me, turn me inside out and haul me back with her. I mean, I wouldn't be able to think.'

She laughs at all this.

'Sounds pretty normal to me,' she says. 'So you want to stay up here a bit longer, then? Be around when your auntie comes out of hospital?'

'I just want to see it through, properly, by myself.'

She gets up.

'Come on then,' she says. 'Let's get it over with before that lot come buzzing round here like a swarm of locusts. Have a word with her myself if you like – make it all sound proper and above board, though why I'm doing this for you I don't know . . . need my bloody head read. . . .'

Listen. She charges in where angels – even Gwennie's – might have been reluctant to tread.

'Is that Mrs Thomson? Jinnie Evans from Bettws here . . . about your daughter, yes, that's right. Not at all, nothing's happened, no, she's fine . . . lovely girl. . . . She's been helping us out here for the last couple of weeks and then her auntie got ill of course. . . . I run a pony-trekking centre – oh, very tiny, nothing to write home about but I'm run off my feet in the season and I can always do with a bit of extra help. . . .

'Of course I would have contacted you sooner but she gave us an address down in Swansea and I saw no reason to question that at the time . . . seemed very straight and above board . . . honest type, your girl . . . didn't realize at the time there were complications. . . . Oh listen, I don't blame you for one minute. . . . I've got two boys and if either of them went off gallivanting halfway across the country. . . . Put your mind at rest now; she's fine – a bit sunburnt but nothing worse . . . heart in the right place, too . . . wants to be around when her auntie comes out of hospital, love her. . . . Oh, I'm sure you would but you know what these kids are like – stubborn as mules, independent . . . wants to do it all herself – mine are just the same.

'Bit of a mam's girl, isn't she? Oh, I said that because she just wants to see her dad – hasn't got the nerve to tackle you yet. . . . They have to get away from us to sort themselves out, I suppose. . . . At least she had the good sense to go to family. . . .'

This unexpectedly patronizing version of my situ-

145

ation both infuriates and amuses me. This woman is clever: she is giving Mum precisely what she needs to hear. I listen in awe and admiration.

'Oh, she's a lot better . . . tough as old boots, our Gwen, though I don't know how much longer it'll last . . . mentally not so hot, no. Look, Mrs Thomson, I'll be frank with you. Social worker down here – funny old girl – she's been making a bit of a fuss about the whole set-up . . . niece turns up but no family – looks bad. No, of course you couldn't . . . it wouldn't have been reasonable to expect it but it will sort things out in more ways than one when one of you does turn up and since Cealie wants to see her dad. . . .

'Oh, I told her you'd understand but she wouldn't believe me. Scared of hurting your feelings, see. . . . Always underestimate us, don't they? I'm sure you'd like a word with her yourself . . . nice talking to you. . . . Oh, we must, yes, I'd enjoy that . . . I'll give her a call . . . Cealie!'

You know, she has got it all wrong: Glyn's talent for acting doesn't necessarily come from his dad's side of the family, does it? So how can someone so perceptive be so insensitive when it comes to her own son? Maybe I am confusing perceptiveness with deviousness. I mean, she has just cleverly shifted the chess pieces in my favour and one of those pieces is my mother. . . .

This is mean thinking and I stop it. Jinnie is on my side, isn't she? Jinnie is my friend.

Ranjit is my friend.

So is Glyn. . . .

Look, I am not naive. I do not expect people to be simple – I am not simple myself – but why oh why do they have to have so many conflicting faces?

146

I think, for instance, of Glyn's provocative dismissal of Louisa: 'Better screw from a hedgehog. . . .' As a male I had accepted that. Not caring much for Louisa myself, it had not been too difficult for me to think of her as something to be used. Now I began wondering if he was saying things like that about me to the girl with the blonde hair.

Deviousness. . . .

I mean, take my dad, running his almost anarchic reading-room for little kids and yet prosecuting poor old Sandra for over-enthusiasm. His own family isn't all that pure and holy if only he knew. I have nicked the odd chocolate bar, made off with a pen that caught my fancy, jumped buses without paying my fare. So has Roz. It is easy. Everyone does it. So why pick on poor old Sandra and turn your own daughter into Public Enemy Number One? Overnight my nice dreamy old dad turned into a middle-class monster – dogmatic, opinionated and so self-righteous that it made me sick. The principle of the thing was all that mattered to him. . . . I just did not know him any more.

And now there is my mother, too, gazing out at me with alien eyes from the pages of those old books.

I sleep badly, thoughts banging about inside my head all night.

Now with the bright sun rimming my eyes I feel strangely exhilarated. There are no sleep pangs this morning, no warm oblivion to leave; I come into today wide awake, clear-headed and possibly even rational.

I do not know for how much longer I am going to be here. Time is closing in on me and soon I will have to sort out my next move. It might even mean going back for a while, I know that, but if it does, I want to feel that it's my own choice and not just something I am stuck with. The little mystery surrounding my mother will probably go on nagging me like an aching tooth. I can't help embroidering on the clues . . . Gareth . . . and Gwen's Rivers of Tears – I mean, was that Mum she was going on about? Sounds dramatic but probably it was nothing – say the wrong thing to me at the wrong time of the month and I can collapse into the weepies myself.

But it is going to bother me, not knowing. . . .

I decide to do something about it. The clear morning light will doubtless show up the whole thing as a heap of kid's pictures and a few lurid notes she probably wishes she had burnt. I have put silly things on paper myself.

With this in mind, I lift down the box and spread out its contents on the dusty linoleum. A couple of old school exercise books might yield something but apart from those it's the same old load of junk. I turn to the scroll. The rolled-up papers are brittle and stiff and the paper itself that ultra-cheap, fibrous stuff they give you at school. I open them carefully but the caked poster paint has long since cracked and flakes of it fall like confetti into my lap.

Three of the paintings are landscapes, crudely done and no big deal – the sort of thing you might expect from a kid with a bit of talent but no training. She seems to have gone in for these tortured silhouettes against garish colours; trees and rocks again but the details which so much impressed me in the drawings lost in the clumsy botch of paint. She often says: I can only draw; my paintings are really

148

just coloured drawings. Now I know just what she means.

The last one baffles me. At first I cannot make it out at all. It is certainly a coloured drawing; you might even call it an elaborately decorated diagram. It's a bit creepy actually. I mean the middle of it is like something you might draw for your Human Biology notebook. A foetus. A baby. Only this baby is the colour of blood. . . .

This baby is the colour of blood. Black brush-strokes mark the lids of its unformed eyes and its umbilical cord coils like a white serpent against a liver-red uterus. The image gets under my skin: it scares me. And the uterus thing hangs in space like a sort of molten planet and she has made plants grow out of its surface – stems and leaves and flowers, daisies and marigolds and little forget-me-nots – a flowery wreath. . . . A wreath, and I am trembling now, shaking, shivering inside my cotton pyjamas. The sun no longer has any warmth for me; it is a cold searchlight and this is what it shows.

You see, I know. Don't ask me how, but I know. Life. Death. She had a child here. . . .

The thick curve of paper curls over itself as if trying to conceal the pain it holds. I let it drop and it rolls up like a shell.

I go on sitting there for a long time, imagining things that may not be true.

Listen. I do not believe in telepathy. I need proof.

I begin systematically sifting through the papers; anything pre-nineteen sixties goes back in the box. I probe the remaining small pile with the needle-sensitivity of shock but there is nothing but trivia.

I turn back to the exercise books, flipping the pages

149

– nothing of any real interest. Then, scrawled across one page, I find it: 'And they call it making LOVE.'

The word LOVE is underlined in red pencil. And then it all comes. . . .

'I can't run away from you . . . nobody wants you but me and I can't, can't, can't. Auntie Gwen says it won't hurt, that she's an expert, her old village wise woman. Well, how would she know anyway, sexless old witch? She wants me to blackmail him into marrying me but that would be awful. . . . Does she do it with knitting needles?'

And across the bottom of the page there is this childish declaration:

'I will have real children one day. I will have a girl and a boy and I will call the boy Justin and the girl Cecilia. Cecilia is the most beautiful girl's name in the world.'

It is like meeting my own ghost. I, Cecilia, am her dreamchild and I mourn for the brother or sister I have lost. . . .

Filled with sadness I walk out in a silver drizzle on to the damp hills, the cool, moist air fresh in my nostrils. Behind this thin veil of cloud the sun lies weeping in a golden pool.

I don't blame her, of course. How could I? I wouldn't want to be stuck with a baby at whatever age she was – fifteen? Sixteen? I mean you make a mistake, and you should have known better; nobody asked you but your body is making a baby. I know. It could have happened to me. And in those days they didn't even have the pill.

The Matthias must have been around then. She has lived in Bettws all her life; a scandal like that and she must have known. I wonder if I can prise it out of her, get past her taboos. Sex? There's dirty. . . .

And my dad – I wonder where he fits into all this? Does he know? Could I ask him? No, of course I couldn't. None of my business, is it? You know, though, sometimes I wonder if she really fancies him at all. I have even wondered how they ever got together in the first place. For one thing, he is serious about literature, but Mum is always turning up with yet another of those self-improvement manuals – listen, if those things really worked, she'd be Prime Minister by now.

I wonder if she secretly dreams about him? Gareth, I mean. . . .

She's very fond of Dad, of course; that's obvious, even to me. I believe it was a publisher friend of Dad's who got her started in the first place. Gratitude's not quite the same thing as love, though, is it? Not to mention passion . . . all that heavy stuff.

I come back to the familiar garden. The apple tree which houses an angel stands dark against an alabaster sky. My sweatshirt is beaded with moisture. I wonder if the Matthias will turn up. I fry an egg, cut some bread, make some coffee and hang about waiting for the car. By half-past three I am certain she is not coming. She has other commitments today. Gwennie will be all by herself and I am sorry.

Listen . . . I have grown old here at Bettws.

15

At four-thirty, for something to do, I walk down to the Evanses. Jinnie comes out to greet me.

'Glad you've come . . . save me a journey. Your Dad rang. Driving down tomorrow morning – be with you in time for lunch.' At the expression on my face she adds: 'Cup of tea or something a bit stronger? Not the end of the world, you know.'

She floats an ice cube in a tumblerful of sweet cider. I sit there in silence, seeing the dandelions mirrored in the mud puddles outside, and watching the sun making gold wire out of the wet straw.

'Won't be the same, though, will it? Nothing will ever be the same again. . . .' My voice is wobbly and for one precarious moment I could break down and tell her everything: the abortion, Gareth (her Gareth?) – the lot.

'Nothing ever is, if you stop and think about it,' she says quietly, and the moment passes. I quickly change the subject.

'Glyn out on a trek?'

She nods. 'Back any minute now, all being well.'

Car tyres scrape across the yard and a horn sounds twice.

'Who's this, then?' She walks across to the open

door and calls out: 'Hullo, Doris, come on in.' She looks back at me. 'Miss Matthias. News about your auntie, no doubt. Let's hope it's good.'

Rows of lilac-rinsed curls frame Miss Matthias's solid, sensible features.

'How's our Gwen then?' I hear Jinnie ask.

'Oh, she'll die with her boots on yet. Out tomorrow, if you please . . . wonderful for her age in spite of everything.' She suddenly spots me hovering round the kitchen door. 'Hullo, Sam,' she says, and immediately checks herself. 'I mean . . . oh dear . . .' and she looks desperately from me to Jinnie.

'Jinnie knows; it's alright.'

'Nothing much anyone keeps from Jinnie Evans for long,' remarks Jinnie tartly. 'What time you picking her up then?'

'Around four.'

'Well, there's a nice coincidence for you.' She sounds pleased with herself. She should. After all, she more or less arranged it. 'There'll be a family car to drive her home in state – she'll be over the moon.'

'Oh yes.' Miss Matthias visibly crumples; she looks like a child whose lollipop has just been snatched away. 'No need for me in that case,' she says stiffly, and I feel really sorry for her.

'But you must come and say hello to my dad.'

'How long is he staying?'

'A day, that's all . . . so that we can get things sorted out a bit.' It's an optimistic guess.

'Mam not coming then?'

'Can't get away.'

'Then you must make the most of each other,' she says brightly. 'Blood's thicker than water, after all; you don't want strangers around at a time like this.'

153

She is even feeling left out enough to add: 'Might be better if you brought up the subject of care, Sam . . . none of my business, really, is it?'

After she has left, I hang around in the hope of seeing Glyn. It is not that there is anything so special about him. I just feel like talking to someone of my own age. I mean, anyone would do – Ranjit, Roz . . . but down here I do not have much choice. I am beginning to feel at least forty.

Like a well-trained puppy, I follow Jinnie round the house and stables, helping whenever I can and hanging back a bit foolishly when I can't. Gwen home tomorrow . . . I feel as if she has been away for weeks. And Dad coming here . . . it's as if things are shaping themselves back into a kind of normality, but I am not reassured. The familiar faces don't look the same to me any more; the familiar script rings false.

So Dad and I will pick up Gwen from the hospital and bring her home. How ridiculous! What a pantomime life has become, with long-lost loves, dotty old ladies and talking angels . . . I suddenly remember the be-spectacled angle down in the churchyard.

'How do you remove felt-tip?' I ask Jinnie.

'Depends what it's on – there's stuff you can buy at the chemist's.'

'It's not on clothes. It's on stone.'

'Stone?'

'The angel in the churchyard.' I explain my theory. 'Auntie Gwennie's got a thing about it.'

' 'course . . . that's where she always stands to do her preaching . . . never occurred to me before.'

'Kids have scribbled rings around its eyes. Looks awful. . . . Might upset her.'

154

'She'd never notice that . . . not in a million years
. . . not from the back of a car.'

'All the same I'd like to clean it up. Before she gets
out.'

'Alright then, let me think. Depends how porous it
is. Vim should do it, and one of those scouring pads.
That and a good dose of elbow-grease.'

'What's that?' I ask naively.

She laughs.

'Power of your elbow, love. Bloody hard slog,
that's what elbow-grease is: best cleaner of all! Rope
in our Glyn, why don't you?'

And at last, here is the sound I have been waiting
for.

They come clattering through the open gate, a
noisy bunch of strangers, laughing, flippant, joking
about the ride. The nervous couple is still around.
They have parked their Metro in the lane; now
they come edging in, conspicuously inconspicuous,
tiptoeing to catch a glimpse of their embarrassed
child.

The blonde next to Glyn sighs like an idiot.

'Never thought I'd make it.'

Glyn shrugs.

'Your riding's not that bad,' he says, but she
modestly shakes her curls.

'Half a dozen times around Glossop Park with a
bunch of kids – that's really all I've ever done,' she
says dismissively. 'I mean, this is for real . . . it's just
fantastic!' I know what she means but I would never
go on about it in that silly breathless way.

' 'lo, Sam.'

My presence acknowledged and forgotten, he
occupies himself with his suddenly awkward group,

155

de-saddling, brushing down, helping people dis-
mount: 'Hold her steady, man . . . hold her . . .
Diawl . . .!' David is there with him, already com-
petent, sure of himself, respected by the others:
nobody treats him like a kid.

'Glyn?' Jinnie bellows from the door. 'I'll see to
that lot for you,' she continues, having forced his
attention. 'You and Sam go get yourselves some tea –
chocolate rolls in the tin! I think Sam needs a bit of
help.'

Help? From him? He can keep it!

I follow him, seething, into the house. I do not
want his help – I can manage perfectly well without
it. Fooled me completely the other evening. Friendship? Easy to take me in with all that faked intimacy –
I wonder how many faces Glyn has? An actor? Oh,
he'll be the greatest!

He plugs in the kettle and brings out a box of tea-
bags.

'Help with what then?'

'Oh, nothing much; I can manage.'

'Well, Mam seemed to think—'

'Your mother exaggerated. Assumes every woman
apart from herself is totally helpless.'

'What's bitten you, then?'

'Nothing.'

We sit down on opposite sides of a wall of silence. I
prod my tea-bag with a spoon. The gulp as I swallow
seems quite deafening.

'What's the matter, Sam?'

'I've already told you – nothing.'

He spoons some sugar into his mug and slowly
stirs.

'What's wrong then, Cealie?'

156

This takes me by surprise.

'Why the Cealie, all of a sudden?'

'Because you're behaving just like a girl.'

'Hardly surprising,' I comment icily, 'since I am one. And tell me, how does a girl behave?'

'Oh . . . being coy . . . playing games . . . not giving a straight answer to a straight question.'

'You're pretty devious yourself.'

'What's that supposed to mean?'

'Behaving like a really close friend one minute, when it suits you, and ignoring me the next. Pretending I'm your kid brother when something more attractive turns up. . . .'

'I was working.'

I am getting a little tired of this self-righteous Welsh innocent.

'You're nothing but a womanizer,' I accuse, deliberately aiming to hurt. 'Just like your dad!' I am angry with both of them – this boy who could so easily be my brother and the man I have never even met.

'You little bitch!' My barb has drawn blood. Now, seeing the pain in his eyes, I am penitent. I went too far. 'What's this bloody job you've got to do?'

'Told you – it doesn't matter.'

'Yes, it does. Tell me.'

I feel a fool but what else can I do?

'I'm going to clean off the graffiti from Gwennie's angel, the one in the churchyard. Vim and a scouring pad, your Mum thinks . . . I can manage.'

He bangs open the cupboard under the sink, hunts around and scoops a few things into a plastic bag.

'Then let's get on with it. You'll be off in a few days then, I presume?'

157

'I don't really know.'

'You know, when I met you, I thought I'd found someone . . . I don't know, sort of wholesome, real. But you're no different from the rest of them, Cealie . . . jealous over nothing . . . attention-seeking—'

'And you,' I retort, 'are just a sexist pig!'

Bearing our mutual rage, we walk grimly down to the village to carry out our chore, two separate and silent people.

In the churchyard, he sets out the contents of the plastic bag in an irreverent line across a neglected mound – two boxes of Vim, a couple of scouring cloths and an orange plastic bowl. Something is missing.

'No water,' I say.

'Why water?'

'Can't actually use this stuff without it . . . didn't you know?'

'Where the hell can we—?'

'Churchyards usually have taps, don't they? For flowers and things.'

'Think of bloody everything, don't you? Just like Mam.'

We hunt around wordlessly, actively disliking each other, carefully avoiding contact. After a while I come across an ancient tap. My triumph is short-lived. I haul on it but nothing happens; it seems to have rusted solid.

With reluctance I call up Glyn.

'Tap but no water . . . can't shift it.'

'Rubbish, man.'

He has a go at it, straining, red-faced, pushing his rage into twisting the handle, strangling the slender metal neck. The handle suddenly gives. Brown, leaf-smelling water gushes out, spilling over our feet. We yell and leap back. I begin to laugh.

'Excalibur!' I shout.

He looks baffled.

'King Arthur's sword – remember? Only he could pull it out of the stone.'

'What's that supposed to mean, then?'

'Only you could turn on the tap.'

He shrugs.

'So make me a king then . . . go on.'

I put my hands on his shoulders.

'Knight first. . . . I dub thee Sir Glyn of the Rusty Tap.'

'Sam. . . .'

I do not know how it has come about but he is kissing my mouth and I am finding the smell of him and the texture of him so heady that I am high as a kite, soaring like an bird . . . or an angel. . . .

16

I haul the crackly, paper-thin sheets, still smelling of mothballs, up around my ears, and lie, watching the golden snowdrift of the one streetlamp animated by the dark and trembling leaves of the rowan.

That damn kiss. . . .

I am not some trembling virgin; I have had my share of kisses. I have none of your romantic illusions and I don't expect a whole string orchestra to strike up, like something from an old movie, at the touch of a bloke's lips. But a kiss coming out of a friendship like this one is a bit different. It doesn't fit. It's as bizarre as a sunflower sprouting out of an apple tree, and a sunflower that grows out of an apple tree would have to be defined as something else.

For amusement, I play around with names. The word 'sunapple' comes into my mind, but it immediately conjures up the freckled rose of his cheek, the sunbleached down on his arms, the smell of his sunwarmed body – in short, all those drooly boy/girl images I had never thought of associating with Glyn.

And there it is again – time, like someone said that night at Pauline's, flowing like water, changing everything, inconstant as a whore . . . I mean, just when I am beginning to grasp things, give them names, some cable twist of the stream throws up new patterns, messing up the old; friendship flows imperceptibly into fancying. Is fancying, then, the death of friendship? I didn't choose this; I didn't want it.

And could the current move in the opposite direction, I wonder. . . .

And there is Mum. What is she doing, gazing past me with the glazed eyes of passion?

And supposing it had been me, that child who had never been born? What if things had been different? What if Mum had said: I am going to have this baby and to hell with you all? What then? No Dad . . . Freda and me, a one-parent family, coping together with all the problems, all the disapproving faces. . . . Might she, then, have turned into some kind of Jinnie?

And tomorrow, Dad will be here. . . .

It sounds silly but I want to impress him.

Already I have worked out a slightly formal lunch – a quiche, if I can get it to work, inside one of Gwen's old cake tins; a salad of sorts, depending on what that dreary shop dredges up; a tin of fruit, perhaps, and even a couple of cans of beer. I know he will be perfectly happy with sandwiches and crisps in the Drovers' Arms, but I want him to see that I can cope.

I am even going to make a WELCOME HOME cake for Gwen . . . eggs, then, and butter; and icing sugar. . . .

Vague fantasies about Glyn drift unwelcome across my shopping list and disintegrate like bubbles when I try to catch them. A solitary car moves down the main road, its radio blaring reggae.

And then there is this boy nonsense. . . .

In order to preserve Gwen's precious illusions, my Dad is going to have to treat me like a son.

It's funny, but I have a sneaking suspicion that he's going to enjoy the whole thing.

I slip imperceptibly into sleep but thoughts go on buzzing inside the hive of my head, constructing the honeycomb of a dream. . . .

I seem to be out in the garden.

' 'lo, Sam.'

Carelessly confident of my fake masculinity, almost brash about it, I am straddling the stone wall.

'Coming riding with us this afternoon then?'

I play it cool. 'Possibly. Depends on her, really,' and I point at Gwennie, standing transfixed beneath the apple tree, her face shining through the round silver pennies of rain.

Glyn slides an arm around my shoulders.

'If you was a girl,' he says, 'I'd fancy you.'

I frown.

'You gay?'

He laughs.

'No. Just observant, that's all,' and cupping my face gently between his hands, he kisses me, slowly and lingeringly.

And the same reaction starts up, my senses on full alert, the throbbing of my heart deafening in my ears, and, 'Glyn,' I think, 'you can touch me anywhere,' . . . her words, her bloody words again, but they seem to form themselves inside my own head as if they were being spoken for the first time.

Our lips, our tongues, taste of apples. . . .

A blast of reggae makes me break away and I think: that damn car again, but the music is coming from somewhere above my head. I look up.

The marble figure sprawls languidly across the branches of the apple tree. Lily robes part to reveal blanched limbs; dreadlocks dangle ultra-violet against heavy swan's wings, stone feathers white as snow. Alabaster eyes, blue-lidded, stare out at me through crude, bright blue spectacles.

'. . . but we cleaned you up,' I stammer.

The angel rolls his eyes.

'Not me, man. Nobody cleans me up . . . that was Gwennie's angel; Gwennie's angel is a virgin pure . . . Cealie's angel, on the other hand,' and he blows lightly over the blue-nailed tips of his white fingers, 'is a bit of a slag, man. . . .'

I am indignant: 'It was only once. . . .' But he just rolls up his eyes and slowly lights up the end of a long, silver joint.

'My eyes see what my eyes see,' he says and laughs.

I pick up his meaning.

'Are you talking about my friend? Were you watching us? Listen, we were only fooling around,' but when I look back for a bit of moral support, Glyn has vanished.

'You should have known better, man. A woman-izer . . . worst womanizer I ever did see. And when you need him most, he's just not there. . . .' He reaches out and plucks a fruit from the tree. 'Have a sunapple.'

The golden orb lies in the palm of my hand. As I watch it, it begins to grow. It grows larger and larger until I can climb right inside it and snuggle down and curl up. And all around me the seeds begin to germinate, the delicate roots fingering the earth, the tender green stems pushing up towards the light. It is like being inside a little planet, rolling and rolling in space, rolling me giddily over and over and over. . . .

Head spinning, I can hear my grandmother's voice.

'Silly little thing got herself into trouble.'

I think of the party and of that boy who means nothing to me. I don't want to have his baby but I wouldn't mind having my baby, just mine, all mine, a baby to cuddle warm in my arms, rock-a-bye baby on the tree top. . . .

'And when the bough breaks?'

Miss Matthias's infinitely sensible face swims above me with its thin halo of curls, like a flushed and watery moon.

'Nice big breath now . . . soon have it out . . . learnt your lesson by now, I hope . . . no more gallivanting for you, my girl. . . .'

A shaky hand – Gwen's, is it? – dabs at my forehead with a handkerchief drenched in cologne.

'Knees apart . . . open your legs. Didn't find it too difficult at the time, did you?'

And a voice rises up out of me.

'No!' it screams. 'No! No! No!'

The sound of my own voice thrusts me into the lightless blue of pre-dawn. My stomach is aching; I have lost the baby, then. . . . But it is only a dream.

Caught between sleep and consciousness, I pad downstairs, turning on lights, touching things, touching myself, and finding with relief everything solid, real and in its usual place.

I open the door and breathe in the fresh, cold air.

The drenched grass is like wet silk. Against a periwinkle sky the apple tree rises, seaweed-green and still, its dark leaves curling and its meagre crop of wizened apples concealed like a miser's hoard against its bulk; no white figures, no Rastafarian angels, nothing supernatural – only a sleepy bird, disturbed, mistakenly singing its dawn song.

Reassured I return to the house – a dream is only a dream – and sort out my stomach-ache on the curved wooden seat of the lavatory. Then, light-headed, cleaned of every emotion, as if the dream had absorbed all my fears into itself, I stumble back to bed and sleep like a child until honeyed sunlight drips warm across my eyelids.

Wide awake, I pull on my crumpled cotton shorts and my baggy shirt.

It is already late and I need to get moving.

After a nightmare, the ordinariness of everything becomes a delight: the flexing and stretching of my silly pink knees as I walk down the stairs makes me giggle; the chill of the kitchen floor against my bare feet is almost a pleasure. I open the back door and a straggle of ants speckles the slate step. Slowly the sun climbs the handles of the heavy-lipped china mugs and tinsels the fluted tea-cups draining beside the sink. The greying locks of the dish-mop steam across the cracked stone. I butter some bread and make myself some tea. Even without last night's disturbance, today will not be easy and already my stomach is back to tying itself into knots. I try to relax, allowing the sun, the milky tea and the buttered bread – nice, simple things – to nurse me into a reverie.

165

But the figure standing at the doorway has walked straight out of my nightmare.

My hands jerk upward and the mug goes crashing to the floor.

'Oh, I am sorry – made you jump out of your skin. I should have knocked but the door was open.' Thick shells of blue and white china lie in a milky mess around my feet. Miss Matthias fusses about, looking for a dishcloth. 'Ought to wear a bell round my neck . . . just popped in to let you know about your auntie.'

But I am somewhere else.

'My mother had an abortion here.' There is simply nothing else I want to say.

Her fidgeting stops. She reaches for a chair and sits down heavily.

'Tell you kids all sorts of rubbish these days . . . no wonder so many nasty things happen.'

'Then it's true.'

She sniffs.

'Who am I to call your mam a liar? No abortion, though, whatever old nonsense she's been telling you. I ought to know, if anyone does.'

'Tell me.'

'You want that sort of dirt, you go and ask your mam.'

'But you helped her, didn't you?'

She sighs.

'Give us a bad name these days, now that it's all legal and they can do it in hospital. We were the ones that took all the risks. . . . Painted us black yet they still came running to us to sort out their little mistakes. I did my best, too, not like some . . . always fussy about cleanliness, see – oh, I could tell you some horror stories if that's what you're after. Her mam,

166

now . . . your gran, must have been . . . sent her up here out of discretion; didn't want that kind of scandal on her hands see . . . wasn't far gone either, poor little mite.'

'And the father?' My voice, like a knife, gouges out the truth.

'No one ever knew and she wasn't saying . . . some school camping trip over Cardigan way so they said . . . some local chancer.'

'Gareth?'

'Gareth, Gryffydd . . . two a penny down here.'

'And you . . .?'

'Never laid a finger on her . . . never had to, see. Worked herself up into such a state it was all over by the the time I came on the scene. Floods of tears, of course, but no more baby . . . never stopped crying; poor old Gwen didn't know what to do with her, not used to that sort of thing. Never saw her again after that . . . stopped coming.' Her voice hardens. 'All ancient history now, water under the bridge. Different world now, isn't it? Don't know you're born, you lot – pleasure without paying the price. . . . If I'd ever wanted to make myself so cheap,' she suddenly blurts out, 'I'd have kept it, no matter what.' Her grief is unmistakable.

I reach out and touch her shoulder but, unused to such physical contact, she shrinks away from me in embarrassment.

I am contrite. 'I'll make you some tea. I'm sorry I upset you but it was something I had to know.'

'Oh never mind.' She relapses back into brightness; her party smile returns. 'Auntie'll be ready for collection by four – that's what I really called in to tell you. Any problem, let me know. I'll be around.' She

167

spoons sugar into her cup. 'Talented girl, your mam
. . . used to do a lot of drawing, and she painted some
quite nice pictures . . . too busy now, I expect, for
that sort of thing.'

'Oh no, it's her job. She illustrates children's books
and does cards and things.'

'Well then,' she announces with satisfaction. 'Not
all bad, see.'

'I'll send you one of her cards if you like.'

'Will you? There's nice – I'll treasure that. . . . You
got her gift, then?'

I think for a moment that she's talking about a
parcel. Then I catch on.

'Can't draw for toffee; my sister's the artist.'

'Two girls then she's got . . . there's lovely . . . I'm
glad.'

'Not always . . . lovely, I mean. We fight like cats
sometimes.' We are suddenly as close as conspirators. 'I've got to go down to the village; doing a
special lunch for my dad.'

'Not much choice in that old shop – like a lift over
to Llanrwst?'

'Don't need much; got it all worked out. If you
could take me down to the shop though. . .?'

'Nice young chap, that Evans boy,' she remarks
archly on the way down. 'Could have been a handful,
those two, with no father.' She nudges me. 'Your dad
know he's got a son yet?'

I shake my head.

'I've still got to break it to him.'

'Then take my advice,' she whispers daringly, 'and
get him a flagon of cider to soften the blow.'

In the shop, the red-haired woman greets me with:
'Old lady any better?'

168

I hold myself stiff and distant from her assumed intimacy. In the gloom of the Post Office enclosure I can see the man, astride a plum-coloured leatherette stool, lopsided over some official-looking document and full of self-importance. I offer them as little as possible. Even my short 'Coming home today,' is uttered with reluctance.

Instead, I concentrate on my list, working through it anxiously, for I will not have time for a second trip.

'Can't sell you any cider . . . not eighteen by a long chalk, are you, dear? Against regulations, see.'

'Don't bother to put that flagon away. I'll have it.'

When I turn round, Jinnie, standing quietly behind me, winks. 'Big day today, isn't it? Wait for me and I'll run you back.'

'Going to fuddle his head with alcohol then,' she comments breezily as we drive up the hill.

'Miss Matthias's suggestion, actually. Haven't told him about the boy thing yet, you see.'

'Miss Matthias? Well, well, well – wonders never cease with you around, do they? Have her knocking it back down the Drovers' Arms any old day now.' She pulls up at the turn-off for the cottage. 'For an encore you can drive this old wreck up to your front door.' She shrugs off my protests with: 'Still got the L-plates in the back. I don't think you're going to do anything daft, though. Taught our Glyn this way but he's down for a few proper lessons now.'

Docile with awe, I follow her instructions, and watch that immense vehicle – I swear it has grown twice as big since she strapped me behind the steering wheel – proceed slowly up the road.

'Well done, Sam,' she says, hauling on the handbrake for me. 'Make a driver out of you yet. Listen. You can tell your dad you've been helping us out and we've been giving you pocket money. Suppose you've been using hers and I don't altogether blame you – you had to eat and so did she – but it don't look very nice, telling him that. If you'd like to make it more businesslike, we'd be only too glad of some help over the next few weeks. Busiest time for us, August – run off our feet. Pocket money, mind; don't expect to get rich out of it. . . .'

I put my box of shopping and my flagon of cider down on the kitchen table.

Funny: when I hugged Jinnie – and what else could I do? – she froze and drew back in exactly the same way as Miss Matthias. I have this strange thought: light and shade are really two opposite sides of the same thing. I mean, I reach out gladly for the sunbeam that is Jinnie and find myself still grasping shadows. . . .

I mix the cake with a mis-shapen fork; no electric beaters in this kitchen. Wasps come to savour the sweetness. Ants, in my short absence, seem to have multiplied. There is a dark side to everything, I think, and reality must have many faces. Even my own image is not fixed; one of these days I shall look into the mirror and meet the eyes of a stranger. . . .

Glyn walks in as I am rolling out the pastry for the quiche and offers me a bouquet of earthy lettuces.

'No good green stuff down the shop, Mam said, and we've got more of these than we can use. Bring your dad down for a drink later on if you like. . . .'

His eyes meet mine.

' 'lo, Sam.'

No kiss, but I am not looking for one. I have learnt

170

that there are no set rules in this game. I mean, you think you are sure but then Life is crouching, round the next corner, all ready to pounce.

You know, I'm beginning to think I like it this way. It is just as well; I have no choice. . . .

As the first and unmistakable car turns into our lane, we twist a cone of paper into a kindergarten angel, and stand it, carefully, in the middle of the unset icing.